After more than thirty years of navigating ministry issues in the same growing church, I can tell you that John Cionca has been used by God to craft a consulting manual to serve Christ's church. It is a guide to healthy biblical evaluation, effective planning, and timely course corrections for every leader in every church at every stage of ministry. **–Larry Adams**, senior pastor, Golden Hills Community Church, Brentwood, California

I lose sleep over the fact that 80 percent of churches are plateaued or declining. John Cionca is not only convinced that heaven wants us to do better, but through leveraging his years of working with many churches, he offers a workable and comprehensive path toward church health and kingdom impact. **–Gene Appel**, senior pastor, Eastside Christian Church, Anaheim, California

I have known John Cionca from my first days at seminary some twenty-three years ago. I was immediately attracted to him and his leadership because of his enthusiasm for practical, biblical ministry. He is uniquely wired to bring high energy to making the church more effective. In *Your Church at Its Best!* he demonstrates that passion again. More than that, he offers many tools to help any church become healthier. This is a book the church needs today and will need in the days to come. **–Jim Barber**, president, Society for Church Consulting

I first became acquainted with John Cionca when I chaired a search committee that hired him as interim pastor. Over the years we have stayed connected as ministry colleagues and as brothers in the Lord. His latest church resource, *Your Church at Its Best!,* is a true treasure chest of wisdom and experience. It is like a condensed package of ministry insights and practices. You can simply add the "water" of your own circumstances, and the odds of your own kingdom impact will be greatly enhanced. What a GIANT gift John's wisdom and enormous experience will be to those who have this masterful guide. –**Jay Bennett**, chairman, National Christian Foundation

Having been in the pastorate nine years before beginning seminary, I remember sitting in Dr. Cionca's seminary class feverishly taking notes, not because I would be tested on the material, but because I knew I would use what I was hearing, not only immediately in my church, but for the rest of my ministry life. His wisdom and practicality were like water in the desert. The foundation for ministry we do at Jacob's Well was taught to me by John and is now released in this wonderful book. I will recommend this great resource to my staff team, fellow pastors, and the church planters I coach and mentor. –**Paul Berthiaume**, lead pastor, Jacob's Well, Eau Claire, Wisconsin

In *Your Church at Its Best!,* John Cionca has brought together into a coherent framework many of the things we know as pastors, but don't consistently apply. The practicality of vision casting, the prioritizing of listening for the Spirit's call, and the encouragement not to chase after the fad of the hour are all relevant. This is a workbook for those practicing "real-life leadership" in all-too-human churches. It gives us hope! If wisdom is the application of insight to life, then *Your Church at Its Best!* is a fresh breeze of wisdom at just the right time. –**John Crosby**, senior pastor, retired, Christ Presbyterian Church, Edina, Minnesota

Your Church at Its Best! Partnering with the Spirit in Ministry is like having a church consultant at your fingertips. Cionca lays a sturdy biblical foundation for church health and then builds a framework with practical examples on each page. Years of ministry experience shine through this resource that will equip pastors for more effective churches. –**David Daniels**, lead pastor, Pantego Bible Church, Fort Worth, Texas

I have been waiting for John to write this book for some time now. There are very few people who have logged as many hours as he has in coming alongside churches to learn from them and to assist them. He is the guy you want to be listening to, I promise. Whether your church is "taking in water" or ready to chart a new course, this book will help you navigate the adventure. –**Randy Frazee**, lead teaching pastor at Westside Family Church in Lenexa, KS, and author of *The Connecting Church 2.0*

Through years of experience in the church and seminary classrooms, John Cionca provides compelling and practical insights for church leaders in *Your Church at Its Best! Partnering with the Spirit in Ministry.* Cionca's model for church health is a must for anyone passionate about the mission of the church today. Climb on board and expand your understanding of how to effectively lead Great Commission movements in and through your local church. –**Justin A. Irving**, director of doctoral studies and professor of ministry leadership, Bethel Seminary, Saint Paul, Minnesota

John does it again. Decades of experience working in the boiler room of churches has given John eyes that see, ears that hear, and the wisdom needed to navigate a way forward—one that leads to vital union with Jesus Christ and results in high impact for God's reputation. –**Joel Johnson**, senior pastor, Westwood Community Church, Chaska, Minnesota

Much has been written recently about church health. Most books focus on a handful of components contributing to the healthy functioning of a church. In John Cionca's *Your Church at Its Best!*, the contemporary church has a manual addressing the full spectrum of church health. From a solidly biblical and theological foundation, Cionca builds on his decades of experience as a pastor, seminary professor, and church consultant. He clearly, concisely, and concretely describes in detail the myriad dimensions contributing to a healthy church in today's challenging context. In addition to many helpful examples and illustrations, Cionca provides specific action steps churches can take to implement the various principles he discusses. *Your Church at Its Best!* will be equally beneficial to those actively involved in building healthy churches, as well as to those teaching in academic settings preparing women and men to be engaged in that task. **–John Lillis**, provost, Grace College and Theological Seminary, Winona Lake, Indiana

Your Church at Its Best! gathers biblical understanding, organizational theory, leadership acumen, and practices of the Spirit into a comprehensive approach to congregational vitality. Drawing on his evangelical roots and his extensive knowledge and experience, Cionca provides church leaders with an excellent, accessible, workable road map to congregational health and effective ministry. Both pastors and lay leaders will find inspiration and wise instruction in its Spirit-filled imagination and clear instruction. **–Roland Martinson**, researcher and author in Christian practice, Luther Seminary, Saint Paul, Minnesota

Cultural shifts are taking place in North America, creating new complexities in ministry. Changing technologies, the collapse of modern Christendom, and the growing ethnic populations are just a few of the new winds of change blowing across the church landscape today. As pastors and other church leaders seek to understand and navigate the changes, John Cionca provides helpful answers in *Your Church at Its Best! Partnering with the Spirit in Ministry.* Based on Cionca's research among five hundred-plus churches and pastors, the book shows church leaders how to sail through the numerous winds of change to become a healthy church. Every church leader should read it and use it to set a biblical direction for their church. **–Gary L. McIntosh**, Talbot School of Theology, Biola University

As an experienced leader and teacher in both the local church and the seminary, I found that John Cionca's *Your Church at Its Best!* is significantly insightful and helpful. I believe church leaders will benefit from this book. Much of its value rises out of its description of sixteen church health factors, and the ideas for application and implementation of those factors in the local church. What is especially helpful is the way John weaves these health factors into one system, using a ship metaphor, so that one sees the parts and the whole in a comprehensive way. This is a good read for any pastoral leader wanting to assess the church and come to wise decisions for the future. **–Hal Pettegrew**, professor emeritus, Lancaster Bible College and Capital Seminary and Graduate School

Anyone who has studied anatomy knows the human body is complex. John Cionca looks at the equally complex church body, and his presentation, while detailed, is clear and helpful, charting a course for the body's health. Everyone within the church, especially leaders, will benefit from *Your Church at Its Best!* **–Marshall Shelley**, director of the doctor of ministry program at Denver Seminary

There is no one I know who understands the inner workings of churches better than John Cionca. Drawing from years of in-the-trenches experience, John provides wisdom and insight for building up and maintaining healthy church dynamics. If your goal is to grow your church into spiritual maturity and ministry effectiveness, this book is for you. –**Mark L. Strauss**, Ph.D., university professor of New Testament, Bethel Seminary

In *Your Church at Its Best! Partnering with the Spirit in Ministry,* John Cionca clearly frames what is needed for a church to be both healthy and missional. He encourages honest reflection, as there is No Vitality without Reality! Moreover, the headings he uses throughout each chapter are incredibly helpful. His approach to identifying healthy missional markers is spot-on. –**Mark R. Stromberg**, superintendent, Northwest Conference of the Evangelical Covenant Church

Filled with real-life, not theoretical, examples, John Cionca lays out his understandings for today's church. While every era looks at things in different ways, the handles he describes are very accessible to all church leaders to apply within their own context and culture. *Your Church at Its Best!* is a quick read that will keep you thinking over and over. –**Dave Travis**, CEO, Leadership Network

Your Church at Its Best!

PARTNERING WITH THE SPIRIT IN MINISTRY

Your Church at Its Best!

PARTNERING WITH THE SPIRIT IN MINISTRY

John R. Cionca
with Leonard G. Goss

Published by Redemption Press, PO Box 427, Enumclaw, WA 98022

Toll-Free (844) 2REDEEM (273-3336)

Redemption Press is honored to present this title in partnership with the author. The views expressed or implied in this work are those of the author. Redemption Press provides our imprint seal representing design excellence, creative content, and high-quality production.

ISBN 13: 978-1-68314-812-8 (Paperback)
978-1-68314-814-2 (ePub)
978-1-68314-813-5 (Mobi)

Library of Congress Catalog Card Number: 2018962105

DEDICATION

This book is dedicated to the board members of Ministry Transitions, Inc. Thank you, Dennis, Doug, Gloria, and Joe for your commitment to our purpose of "helping leaders and churches chart their future." (JRC)

I dedicate this work to Lia Fei, Madeline Marie, Sylvia Liying, and Shelby Jean, my four beautiful granddaughters. (LGG)

PROLOGUE

Why do some churches flounder, while others thrive? Why are some stagnant or declining, while others are vibrant and growing? Many think that, like real estate, church health has to do with location, location, location. Others counter church health is pastor, pastor, pastor.

Admittedly, demographics do play a significant part in congregational growth. A visible, attractive, and comfortable campus is welcoming. A visionary pastor who does a great job with relevant, biblical communication is appealing. Yet these factors alone do not explain why some congregations thrive and others decline. We can all name congregations, for example, that even with their large campuses and good preachers, are nevertheless experiencing decline.

Consider this: What would your church look like running on all eight cylinders? If your church was at its best, what would be happening that is not happening now? If your congregation was experiencing maximum health, what would it be doing? Can you envision a better tomorrow for your church? Can it grow in missional effectiveness? The answer is a definite *yes*.

The resource you are holding is the result of my twenty-year study of church health. It is gleaned from over five hundred congregations and pastors I have assisted as executive director of Ministry Transitions, Inc., a Christian ministry dedicated to helping church leaders and churches plan their future. In addition, the work draws from the best insights from colleagues and church consultants used as resources in my seminary course on congregational systems. For that class I require students to compare the health factors identified by notable church analysts. More specifically, drawing from six popular writers—George Barna, Kennon L. Callahan, William M. Easum, Stephen A. Macchia, Dan Reeves, and Christian A. Schwarz—they merge and redact the authors' identified factors into one composite list of sixteen distinct contributors.

To explain the interrelatedness of those sixteen health factors, I selected the model of a ship for illustrative purposes.

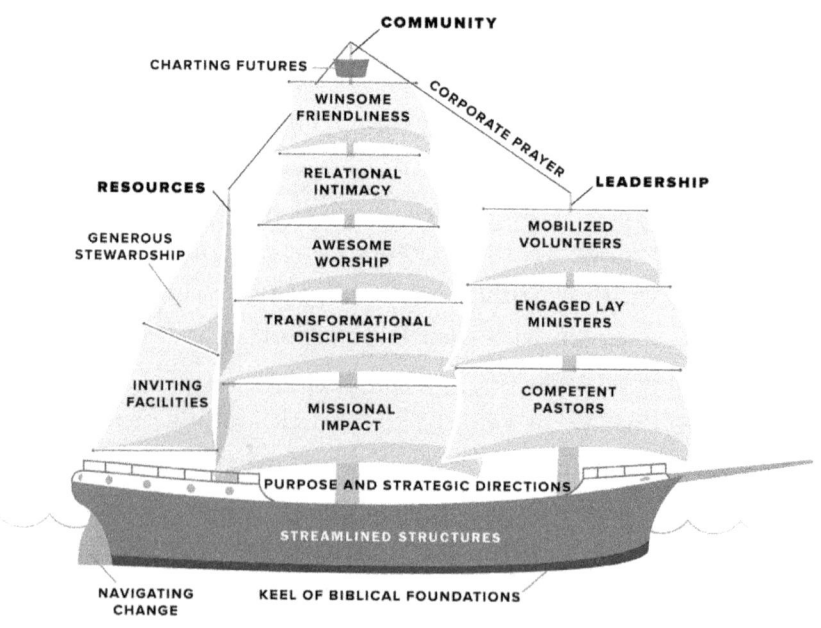

For a successful ocean voyage, all aspects of a ship are important: the structure, bridge, masts, sails, rigging, and rudder must all be in working condition for safe travel. This is also true for successful ministry, which requires four essential elements: structural integrity, effective leadership, dynamic community, and essential resources. These four rudiments comprise the basic sections of this book.

The first part of this book has to do with the structural integrity of ministry. Setting a course for church health demands a structural integrity built on the interdependency of biblical foundations, streamlined structures, purposeful and strategic direction, the charting of futures, navigational change, and corporate prayer. Each of these components represent the six chapters in part one of the book.

Part two has to do with effective leadership, and this is illustrated by one of the ship's three masts. On the mast of effective leadership are three sails, and the chapters in this section of the book detail the necessity of mobilized volunteers, engaged lay ministers, and competent pastors.

A second mast on the ship illustrates part three, dynamic community. Five sails, or church health factors, are related to a congregation's community life, which includes both nurture and outreach. The chapters in this part of the book unpack the importance of winsome friendliness, relational intimacy, awesome worship, transformational discipleship, and missional impact.

The fourth and final section of the book covers essential resources, and this is pictured as the third mast on the ship. Essential resources enable ministry to happen, for they make possible the requisite staff and programs essential to strengthen the church and serve the community. The two sails on the third mast of leadership are generous stewardship and inviting facilities.

For proper functioning, all constituent parts of the ship are critical for safe and successful travel. Congregational health is possible only when all constituent parts of the church are functioning at full capacity.

A streamlined structure (good governance) without a rudder (the ability to change) makes reaching our destination (mission) impossible. If our sail of facilities is fully unfurled, we will still not have enough hands on deck to see much kingdom growth if our sail of volunteerism is barely open. We may have a sail of worship that is awesome (raised high), but if our sail of missional impact is down, our people will propel themselves in a circle without reaching new land.

A congregation's health is more complex than just the effectiveness of its pastor or the advantage of a prime location. Many other factors help or hinder a congregation from realizing its potential. Another thing to keep in mind is that we are not victims, unable to improve our church's missional effectiveness. We *can* make better decisions (bridge), retain a greater number of visitors (relational intimacy), increase our giving (generous stewardship), and draw people into deeper levels of service (engaged lay ministers). We *can* improve our church's ministry and take charge of its destiny, irrespective of the waters in which we are sailing (local demographics).

Before considering individual church health factors, however, let me comment on the format of my presentation. In the book I will say that *this* is more important than *that*. For example, when it comes to volunteerism, I believe it is more about retention than recruitment. Therefore, retention is more important than recruitment. Regarding relational intimacy, it is more important to connect new people to other new people than it is to connect new people to core members. The same this-and-that factor is true for generous stewardship, which is more about commitment than capacity. I mention this to say it is never totally *not about this*. It is just more about *this*, than it is about *that*.

With that in mind, let the journey begin.

CONTENTS

PROLOGUE xiii

Part One: **STRUCTURAL INTEGRITY** 19
Chapter 1:   BIBLICAL FOUNDATIONS 21
Chapter 2:   STREAMLINED STRUCTURES. 29
Chapter 3:   PURPOSE AND STRATEGIC DIRECTIONS 35
Chapter 4:   CHARTING FUTURES 45
Chapter 5:   NAVIGATING CHANGE 55
Chapter 6:   CORPORATE PRAYER 63

Part Two: **EFFECTIVE LEADERSHIP** 71
Chapter 7:   MOBILIZED VOLUNTEERS 73
Chapter 8:   ENGAGED LAY MINISTERS 85
Chapter 9:   COMPETENT PASTORS 93

Part Three: **DYNAMIC COMMUNITY**. 101
Chapter 10:   WINSOME FRIENDLINESS. 103
Chapter 11:   RELATIONAL INTIMACY 111

Chapter 12:   AWESOME WORSHIP 119
Chapter 13:   TRANSFORMATIONAL DISCIPLESHIP 131
Chapter 14:   MISSIONAL IMPACT 139

Part Four: **ESSENTIAL RESOURCES** 149
Chapter 15:   GENEROUS STEWARDSHIP 151
Chapter 16:   INVITING FACILITIES 165
Chapter 17:   NEXT STEPS 173

Appendix A: SHIP MODEL FOR CHURCH HEALTH 177
Appendix B: WAYS TO SUPPORT AND RECOGNIZE VOLUNTEERS . . 179
Appendix C: CHURCH HEALTH ASSESSMENT 183

ABOUT THE AUTHORS 185

PART ONE

STRUCTURAL INTEGRITY

CHAPTER 1

BIBLICAL FOUNDATIONS

KEEL OF BIBLICAL FOUNDATIONS

Sailing vessels require a keel for stability. From the surface, we might not even see the keel, but it is essential to keep the ship upright because it is the main structural element extending along the ship's bottom. In our representation, the keel is a congregation's Biblical Foundations. The biblical foundations of any congregation consists of its most basic beliefs. This would include all their essential doctrinal beliefs, including the core biblical mandates defining their ministry. Put another way, the biblical foundations are what we stand for, what is in our DNA. Our biblical foundations are our nonnegotiables.

Some churches have a deep keel, embracing many beliefs as critical to their effectual functioning. They go to the wall on what they consider essential doctrinal issues, polity issues (church governance), and practical issues, such as church program priorities and who can serve in certain roles. But if the only people who are comfortable in our churches are premillenialists, dichotomists, KJV-only users, or devotees of a certain style of preaching, then our deep keel will have limited appeal and limited outreach. The perception of this church is more discriminatory than inviting.

On the other hand, churches without biblical foundations face great challenges. I once worked with a congregation that identified itself as "a pilgrim people on a spiritual journey." I wondered what this could mean and inquired of the pastoral staff: "Could the Mormons also say that?" One pastor responded, "I guess so." "Could the Jehovah's Witnesses say the same?" "I guess so." "Could Muslims at a local mosque say that?" The hesitant response was the same: "I guess so." Their keel ran very shallow. While the church provided spiritual seekers easy entrance, people just as easily drifted away, ending up in congregations with more clearly articulated distinctives.

When considering the health factor of biblical foundations, three principles assist us with determining our nonnegotiables: core beliefs are more important than systematic theology, revelation is more important than enculturation, and infusion is more important than declaration.

Biblical Foundations Are More about Core Beliefs than Systematic Theology

First off, biblical foundations *are* about systematic theology, since every truth statement affirmed from Scripture is important. Nevertheless, the foundations are more about the core beliefs a church embraces that makes it both stable and agile at the same time.

Take membership as a specific example. A church that accepts people into membership based on a faith statement alone has a modest keel. On the other hand, a church requiring a faith statement, believer's baptism by immersion, a commitment to tithing, and a public testimony before the congregation, has a deeper keel. A solid commitment to Jesus Christ as Savior and Lord is essential for membership in most churches (a stable and agile keel), but churches requiring, say, a public testimony before the whole congregation, are not as agile.

All theology is important, but core beliefs define a congregation. Bethlehem Baptist Church in Minneapolis, Minnesota, embraces the whole counsel of the Word of God, but what they are known for is their emphasis on God's sovereignty. North Coast Church in Vista, California, embraces Evangelical Free Church polity, but they are best known for their small-group ministry. Their senior pastor says they ruthlessly guard against anything detracting from their people doing life together in community. Willow Creek Community Church in Illinois teaches from the entire Scripture, but one learns very quickly that what drives the church is the theme from the parable of the lost son: lost people matter to God. "This son of mine was dead and is alive again; he was lost and is found" (Luke 15:24).

The greater the list of theological nonnegotiables, the more potentially exclusionary a church becomes to seekers. Contrariwise, too few theological nonnegotiables can mean more confusion for people. What beliefs make up your church's core biblical foundations? Do they provide stability, yet permit agile travel?

Biblical Foundations Are More about Revelation than Enculturation

A congregation's belief system must not be determined by what is fashionable in society. Take for example the role of women in ministry, a controversial issue among Christians. In seminary, students may have a theoretical discussion on the role of women in leadership. In a local church, however, either women are on the board, or they are not—depending on the church bylaws.

If church leadership adopts an egalitarian position regarding women in leadership, it should not do so because women are now in corporate executive positions, or because the church desires the perception of being welcoming of women. Instead it should articulate that "Based on these Scriptures and for these reasons, we believe the gifts of the Spirit and the offices of the church are open to men and women equally." Alternatively, if a congregation adopts a complementarian approach, it would affirm that "Based on these Scriptures and for these reasons, we believe the office of elder is appointed to men only."

How baby boomers or millennials *feel* about women in executive church leadership is not the point. Culture is important, but biblical foundations are more about revelation than assimilating popular culture.

Another hot-button cultural issue in America today is the legalization of same-sex marriage, which has caused division within mainline churches for many years. Pastors and congregations wishing to welcome the LGBT community generally affirm same-sex marriages. Other churches seem exclusionary when they say, "Repent of your sin, and then you can come to our church." Many evangelical churches welcome all people who want to know more about the Lord, but they do not vacillate when it comes to the Bible's teaching that marriage is between one man and one woman.

To reiterate, a congregation's position on any issue should not be built on popular tastes or current fashions, but on its understanding of Scripture. As theologian Martin Marty observed, "To survey the unchurched world and ask what we should be doing in our churches, is to ask the least informed about the faith to determine its direction."[1] Biblical foundations are the doctrinal nonnegotiables for which the church stands, and they must originate from scriptural revelation, not culture.

---

1   Martin E. Marty, *Newsweek*, August 9, 1993, 48.

Biblical Foundations Are More about Infusion than Declaration

Typically, churches have doctrinal statements which they have personally established or have adopted from their denomination or association. What is most important is not necessarily what one finds in a church constitution, but what people know and embrace. Nor is it what those in the membership class have to affirm, but what they actually believe.

Biblical foundations are more about infusing the faith than declaring it. Many congregations believe that every church member is a minister. Yet I know only a few churches so infused with this belief that members would uniformly say they were all about serving in the name of Jesus.

Sierra Madre Congregational Church in California publicizes their beliefs on their Web site, yet their members all understand they are part of a church where "every member is a minister." Personal volunteerism is in the DNA of this congregation. Similarly, both Fellowship Bible Church in Arkansas and the Dream Center in California have full doctrinal statements, yet they are known for their compassion, outreach, and neighborhood ministries. Their people know spiritual development thrives when serving others.

In summary, when talking about our theological nonnegotiables, no one can be everything to everybody, and we must not try for universal appeal. We can be flexible in outreach and events, but never in our core beliefs. A good keel on a ship gives it stability, but not drag; it provides agility without compromise. Foundationally, this is the only way.

Hoisting the Sails

Here are some ways congregations can strengthen their biblical foundations:

CONCENTRIC CIRCLES

A church in New England uses three concentric circles to describe their biblical foundation. The *inner circle* represents the key doctrinal and ministry values that all professional staff and lay leaders must unwaveringly embrace. Examples of the key or essential beliefs are the infallibility of Scripture and the substitutionary atonement of Christ. The *middle circle* represents the beliefs and practices that are preferred for leadership chemistry. A leader may have a conviction regarding, say, women elders, yet they can still serve a church holding a different position from their own. The *outer circle* represents preferences, beliefs, and issues on which Christians differ. These preferences are non-issues for the congregation. An example of this might be the private practice of speaking in tongues.

DISSOLUTION EXERCISE

A Midwest congregation pondered whether to relocate—or consider dissolution and releasing people to join churches closer to their homes. Their concern was for the neighborhood. Would the neighborhood feel the loss if the church left? Each congregation should ask whether it would actually matter to anyone if they closed their doors. That is the sort of question that will give insight to church identity.

KISS EXERCISE

The acronym KISS stands for "Keep it simple, stupid." Can a church doctrinal statement be edited to maintain distinctives while presenting them in a simpler way? By shortening or combining doctrinal declarations, can the full statement be reduced by 50 percent? Usually, the more tidy a doctrinal summary, the more useful it is.

The Big Three

A valuable exercise is identifying the three to five primary scriptural themes underlying the heart of ministry. Approach it this way: If you had to go to the wall for theological beliefs, what would they be?

Vision Casting

Vision leaks. That is why many pastors have an annual state-of-the-church message to recast the church's purpose. A congregation's foundational beliefs can be restated and refreshed through such a message, as well as through other sermons and presentations on the church's Web site.

Vision Yeasting

The idea behind vision yeasting is introducing vision through personal and small-group opportunities. Through one-on-one sharing, a leader can unburden his or her heart, answer questions, and offer challenges. Borrowing from Deuteronomy 11:19, vision yeasting can help infuse the church's vision by "talking about them when you sit at home and when you walk along the road, when you lie down and when you get up." Regular vision yeasting can produce greater results than an annual message.

CHAPTER 2

STREAMLINED
STRUCTURES

STREAMLINED STRUCTURES

KEEL OF BIBLICAL FOUNDATIONS

Earlier in ministry I served a church with three boards—a deacon board, a Christian-education board, and a trustee board. The Christian-education board recommended hiring a full-time youth pastor. The deacon board agreed the present part-time youth director role should be increased to a full-time pastoral position. The trustee board voted not to fund it. Unfortunately, in that congregation, all the boards were equal, and none of them had authority over any other. I present this as a great example of a non-streamlined structure. In the ship model we have been using to picture successful ministry, the shape of the ship itself—its Streamlined Structure—refers to its governance, its decision-making process.

When considering the health factor of streamlined structures—the shape of the church—four principles assist us: permission is more important than control, doing is more important than deciding, people are more important than the system, and personal ministries are more important than institutional programs.

Streamlined Structures Are More about Permission than Control

How is your church organized? When someone wants to start a ministry, can they do it on their own? Or must they go to a committee, the pastor, or the church board for permission? Generally, it is conceded that a good streamlined structure should only require one level up for decisions. If people have to go up more than one level, discouragement can set in, and with discouragement comes lost interest. The challenge is how to release people to do ministry in freedom, yet with supervision.

A widely known pastor related that while his father was not a believer, he did many things really well in parenting. One thing his father did was to use *yes* rather than *no* as his default answer. Rather than force his kids to make a case for approval to go to a neighbor's house, he would say *yes*—unless there was a good reason not to.

This default practice of approval also works well for churches. Why should someone with a workable dream not be able to go for it? Streamlining the structure of the church does not mean giving up board approval or staff oversight. What it does mean is minimizing the approval process and freeing people as much as possible to engage in ministry.

Streamlined Structures Are More about Doing than Deciding

A smooth-running church is focused more on doing than deciding. I once advised a church with a youth committee comprised of parents working in the program. Their operation was smooth, and their ministry impactful. In another congregation, however, the youth advisory team consisted of a few parents not serving as volunteers. They used their committee role to keep a close watch on the pastor and youth-staff volunteers who ran the program these parents dictated. In this second case, the organizational structure was all about this group of parents supervising and deciding rather than doing. It caused challenges and, quite often, conflict.

In a healthy organization, the deciders are also the doers. I have found that a youth-ministry leadership team is best comprised of those directly engaged in the actual youth ministry. Bring on the elder-board leaders who have already distinguished themselves through service in other areas of ministry. One megachurch I have consulted with has an executive pastor (who is primarily in a management role) who is also responsible for senior adult ministries. At that church, the philosophy is that no one, including professional staff, just supervises the work of others. Everybody has program responsibilities.

Good church governance—good church decision-making—does not allow decisions to be made one month, only to inquire month after month if anything has been done about it yet. It is more about accomplishing things than making decisions.

Streamlined Structures Are More about People than the System

If we want healthy churches that move forward and grow, it is more important to know who leaders are personally than what they are called constitutionally. A friend recently became a senior pastor of a midsize congregation, and the first thing he did was initiate a change in the wording of the church constitution. It is true that some structures are more streamlined than others, but why revise the church constitution as the first order of business? Why waste goodwill on this issue, especially in a new ministry?

In the final analysis, if a church operates with an elder board, which is then changed to a church counsel, nothing much has changed unless the people serving in office are also changed. A deacon board full of cranky deacons that is renamed an elder board with the same people will not help the situation, unless the cranky leaders themselves are replaced. It is all about good leaders. People are more important than the system in place. Another way to say this is that with the right people, almost any structure will work.

Granted, some church structures are better—more streamlined—than others. Many prefer the shape of the church ship to be teams that inform and work with the board. Others have different ideas regarding church governance and decision-making. Let us not forget that in the end, people who lead trump the structure in which they serve.

Streamlined Structures Are More about Personal Ministries than Institutional Programs

Personal ministries are more important than institutional programs. It is demotivating for a believer to view his or her service as merely filling a program need. In youth work, for example, we ought to see not only the youth program, but also the team of people touching the lives of students. These are genuine Christians ministering in the Lord to influence young people, not merely human resources filling program slots. We need to see the team as Christ's followers using their giftedness to disciple youth on behalf of the church.

Many people think if their church only had more programs they could be more effective. That is highly unlikely! It is not the number of programs, nor the nature of the programs that make churches effective. Healthier congregations are the ones that equip and release more people to serve others. That is the solution in a nutshell.

The health factor of streamlined church structure requires inviting people to serve rather than coercing them to serve. It is about empowering Spirit-led servants to use their God-wiring to impact others, whether in an existing program or a new venture.

Hoisting the Sails

Here are some ways a congregation can streamline its structure:

Outsiders' Feedback

Most churches want honest feedback on their congregation, especially on how they come across to visitors. Many actually pay guests, some of them unchurched contacts, to visit and offer critiques of various aspects of the service. A focus group concerned with this type of evaluative or corrective information can be extremely valuable.

DEPTH Analysis

The acronym DEPTH is used to help people discern potential areas of spiritual service. Their *dreams* or *desires* can reveal what their hearts tell them about what sort of service they might like to try. Their *experiences* illuminate what accomplishments give them a sense of joy (internal confirmation) and a sense of recognition from others (external confirmation). Their *personality* wires them for some jobs more than others, preparing them by virtue of their level of extroversion/introversion, dominance, pace/patience, and conformity. Their *talents* show what ministry opportunities they are prepared for. People good with numbers, or skillful in a sport, or proficient in an instrument can all express those gifts and talents on behalf of others. And lastly, the *Holy Spirit* gives gifts, open doors, closes doors, and surprises along the journey.

COMMUNITY-NEEDS ASSESSMENT

In thinking about streamlined structures, we must remember that Christ followers can also serve outside the church. Perhaps their passion is for lost people, or their giftedness does not match existing program positions. The needs of a local community are more comprehensive than a local church's program, yet a congregation can impact their neighborhood through, among other areas, teaching ESL classes (English as a second language), assisting with income-tax preparation, providing foster care or babysitting, or helping with transportation needs. Each church can survey its community to see which of the hundreds of needs their volunteers might meet.

CHAPTER 3

PURPOSE AND STRATEGIC DIRECTIONS

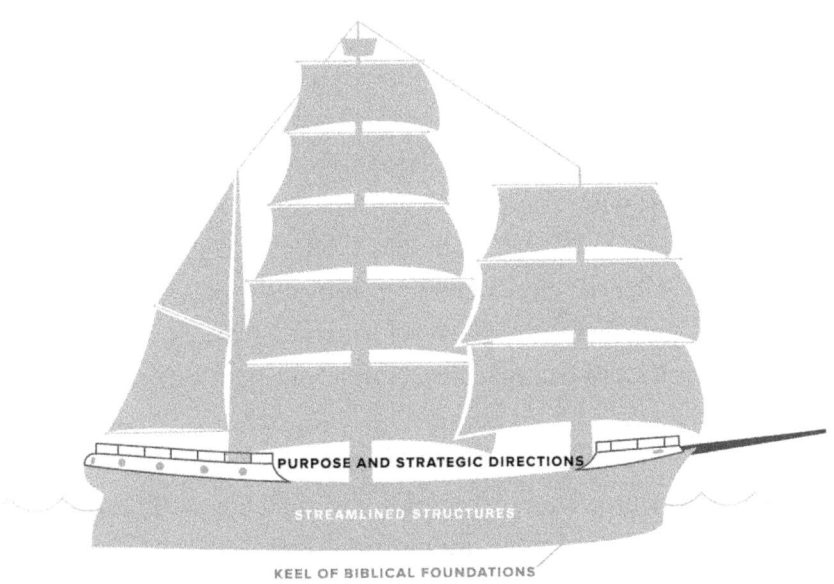

PURPOSE AND STRATEGIC DIRECTIONS

STREAMLINED STRUCTURES

KEEL OF BIBLICAL FOUNDATIONS

As I have said, a successful ocean voyage requires that all aspects of a ship be in working order for safe travel. This is just as true for successful ministry. Thus far we have considered two factors contributing to congregational health: biblical foundations and streamlined structures. The keel (biblical foundations) both stabilizes the ship and makes it nimble, while the shape of the ship (streamlined structures) determines how efficiently a church cuts through the water. The structure is holistic; the keel and the hull cannot be separated.

Now we move to the bridge of the ship, which is where maritime decisions are made. This is also the place where, in our model of a ship, a church's Purpose and Strategic Directions are determined. I intentionally use the word *purpose* rather than *mission* or *vision*. I know the conceptual difference between mission and vision, for I teach in the field of leadership studies. Yet I know the two words confuse many people. A friend who is a corporate consultant was the president of an international company. I asked him the difference between a mission statement and a vision statement. He informed me that "I think all of that is the emperor's new clothes. Just draw me a bull's-eye of what you want to accomplish, and then what you are going to do to hit it. Tell me your *purpose* and what you will do to accomplish it. It's that simple!"

In my work with churches, I give the same advice. What is your purpose? Why do you exist? Why has God placed your church in this community? What do you want to accomplish for Christ's kingdom? A moving target is hard to hit, so we must state clearly and simply our church's purpose and strategic direction. Once that is clear, we can then determine the best ways to accomplish our goals.

When considering the health factor of a church's purpose and strategic directions, four principles should be noted: Purpose and strategic directions are about the Spirit's empowerment, about annual initiatives, about specific outcomes, and about missional impact.

Purpose and Strategic Directions Are More about the Spirit's Empowerment than a Church's Cleverness

At this point in your reading you know the direction of this book. A critical factor of church health is presented, and each chapter concludes with ways to strengthen that area of ministry. But before we go further, it is important to reemphasize the big picture. In the Old Testament, God declares: "'Not by might nor by power, but by my Spirit,' says the Lord Almighty" (Zech. 4:6). The New Testament documents Jesus elaborating: "You will receive power when the Holy Spirit comes on you; and you will be my witnesses in Jerusalem, and in all Judea and Samaria, and to the ends of the earth" (Acts 1:8). While *Your Curch at Its Best* presents an analysis of church health and offers strategies we can implement to improve ministry effectiveness, the overriding truth is that it is Christ who builds his church (Matt. 16:18), and that it is the Spirit of Christ who ultimately produces ministry fruitfulness (John 15:1–16).

The apostle Paul provides a great example of keeping the right perspective when he explains, "To this end I strenuously contend with all the energy Christ so powerfully works in me" (Col. 1:29). The Apostle served with passion and diligence. But it wasn't his genius, insightfulness, or perseverance that built the church. It was his dependency on the Spirit of Christ and his following the Holy Spirit's leading that produced transformation—in Paul himself, and in the many congregations he served. It is little wonder, therefore, that he admonished others to "Walk by the Spirit" (Gal. 5:16), "Keep in step with the Spirit" (Gal. 5:25), "Do not grieve the Holy Spirit of God" (Eph. 4:30), and "Be filled with the Spirit" (Eph. 5:18).

As you continue reading about our part of ministry effectiveness, let us not lose sight of the bigger picture of God's part in building Christ's church. Let us ask the Spirit of Christ to guide us in every way as we assess our congregations and strategize to expand their kingdom effectiveness.

Strategic Direction Is More about Annual Initiatives than Programmatic Entitlements

Do we have Sunday school at our church? Why? Do we have Kid's Zone, Adventure Club, or Promise Land? One hopes our churches have these types of programs for reasons other than "we had them last year," and the year before that, and so on ad infinitum. Ministry programs should not be entitlements, carried along year after year, but rather events carefully chosen by our leaders as specific activities (arrows) to hit best our church's purpose (bull's-eye).

When we determine whether we have lived up to our purpose and strategic direction, we should reuse effective arrows and discard the rest. Professional golfers no longer use the hard fine persimmon woods for driving. Today's titanium composite drivers outdistance those classics by over one hundred yards. Similarly, today's travelers would be foolish to use a 1970s-era road atlas for cross-country travel. Instead, they input the destination into a GPS device to receive current directions from satellite signals far above the Earth's surface. Any congregation serious about their call as witnesses for Christ in their community will only use activities or programs that are most effective *today*.

A congregation aiming to maximize its impact establishes annual ministry initiatives. Unfortunately, in many churches—perhaps in most churches—even pastors and executive staff are not held accountable for annual initiatives. Our churches would be much more productive if more leaders were required to detail, "These are the seven things I will accomplish this year." Strategic direction is more about annual initiatives than perpetuating programs.

Strategic Direction Is More about Outcomes than Goals

A goal is a desired result, something aimed at. An outcome is a finished accomplishment. Let me illustrate: In my consulting, churches want to know what I will do for them. I could tell them I will do this and that, and this and that. Those would all be important goals, but not as important as defining the outcome by saying, "At the end of our time together, you will have a complete ministry audit of programs, staff, and facilities, with a set of recommendations for church growth." Or if I am consulting with a church pastoral-search committee, I might say, "You will be presented with three 'finalist'-level prospects with references and assessments." How I work my network or where I post the position is not really the issue, because what churches ultimately want is the opportunity to choose a pastor from a narrow field of highly qualified, vetted clergy. Therefore, when considering the health factor of church strategic directions, outcomes are more important than goals.

By establishing program initiatives, churches define what will be achieved by the end of the month, quarter, or year. A possible outcome for a youth group might be stated like this: "By the end of August, we will have twenty new students in our senior high ministry, twenty students who are able to share their faith, ten students serving in a short-term mission, and fifteen students working once a month in a community ministry." These initiatives are clear and measurable.

I once advised a church with an aging congregation (two out of three adults were over age seventy) wanting to strengthen the area of worship. We began by brainstorming different ways they might hoist the worship sail. From their list of forty-two possibilities, they chose nine initiatives to accomplish over the coming year. One initiative they selected was producing large-print bulletins. Because their auditorium was very bright with floor-to-ceiling stained-glass windows, the second initiative they chose was getting rid of their dim front projection system and moving to rear projection.

The congregation selected three initiatives they could accomplish within ninety days, such as producing the large-print bulletins (which only took two weeks). Then they identified three additional outcomes, all slated for a 180-day turnaround. Finally, they picked three initiatives they would complete by the end of one year. The church's platform reconstruction was one of these 360-day outcomes. Because the chancel was deemed pretty sacred to some, and because new funding was required to accomplish the reconstruction, a longer completion time was set for this outcome.

Remember, an outcome is a finished accomplishment. If church leadership says, "We want to be a friendlier church—that's our goal," how will they know if they reach this outcome? Again, the goal must be measurable. Strengthening strategic direction is about defined outcomes.

Strategic Direction Is More about Missional Impact than Institutional Caregiving

Strategic direction is about annual initiatives and defined outcomes, and it is also more about missional impact than institutional caregiving. Prioritizing a missional focus—keeping an outward look to the harvest—will surface several times in these chapters. More specifically, the chapter on the bottom sail on the mast of community, "Missional Impact," will examine this priority in greater depth. For now, however, we note that a missional mindset begins on the bridge.

The first thing I want to know when a church calls me for consulting is whether they see their purpose as nurturing a group of Christians to reach their community for Christ, or whether they see their purpose as reaching their community with the gospel—and doing whatever is necessary to accomplish this. Do you see the difference? Churches holding the first view may never get into their neighborhoods. A flock is never nurtured enough. Churches keeping the main thing—the Great Commission—always keep the harvest in view. That is what Jesus was all about. Missional impact counts more than institutional caregiving.

Strategic direction is not about "doing church better." Directional decision-making (from the bridge) primarily must be about making the greatest kingdom impact. Of course churches must care for the people within—the other ninety-nine can still feed in the pasture—but strategic direction is more about missional impact than institutional caregiving.

Hoisting the Sails

Here are some ways a congregation can clarify its purpose and strategic directions:

PURPOSE CLARIFICATION

There are times in a congregation's life cycle when the church's purpose needs clarification and a new direction is required. To tack in a new direction, some churches take a bottom-up approach by considering their own unique history, resources, and community demographics. Other churches take a top-down approach by studying the mission and vision statements of other congregations, and then adopting a statement that fits and energizes their own situation. After all, they figure, we are all part of the Great Commission and the building of the Kingdom, so why not use a proven bull's-eye from a sister congregation? Whatever method a congregation chooses to revisit their purpose and strategic direction, a periodic review is advised.

STAFF LISTENING DAYS

Constance Free Church gives their staff two days away every six months to individually listen to what God may be telling them about their particular ministry. Their church has regular staff meetings and annual off-site planning meetings, but in addition, each ministry leader is given staff listening days to connect with God specifically about the work he has given them to do. These special listening days are in addition to study breaks, and they are not used as planning times. Nor are these days counted as vacation time. Rather, they are set aside for busy leaders to slow down and sense how God may be guiding. Sometimes, while listening to the Lord's voice, the days away confirm a present ministry direction. At other times, however, new thoughts and new possibilities come to mind.

LISTENING EXERCISES

Listening development is very important. Decision effectiveness is limited or enhanced by how well team members can really "hear" one another. Listening and hearing are not the same. When someone is trying to communicate with us, they want to feel they are talking *with* us and *to* us, not *at* us. To help establish strong and effective communication, we need good listening skills.

Listening inventories, books, and articles on how to sharpen our listening skills to become attentive and empathetic listeners are available at stores and on the Web. There are also college-level courses on conscientious listening. Common listening mistakes, such as letting the phone interrupt, not making eye contact, selective listening, holding side conversations with others, interrupting, jumping to conclusions, and so forth, are worth periodic review.

CONFLICT RESOLUTION EXERCISES

There is good conflict and there is bad conflict. In clarifying a congregation's purpose and establishing strategic initiatives, conflict can be favorable when ideas are challenged and assessed. In other words, we should be open to respectfully challenging our team members, because when we always agree, for the sake of being agreeable and for avoiding confrontation, the results can be mediocre at best. The best decisions usually surface after several positions are considered. Conflict enables us to be creative in our problem-solving, and it helps us broaden our resolution skills. Attacking a person is never helpful, but critical analysis of a person's ideas can benefit the whole team in helping choose the best solution. Resources are also available to help ministry teams develop conflict resolution abilities.[2]

COMMUNITY-NEEDS ASSESSMENT

Some people prefer serving in ministry opportunities outside of the church. Possibly their giftedness does not match existing program positions inside their church. Their passion may be for lost people, who

---

2   http://conflict911.com/resources/Exercises_and_Training_Activities_To_Teach_Conflict_Management/.

usually do not frequent church services. A congregation can impact their neighborhood in hundreds of different ways, like volunteering to tutor students, assisting with a work project, providing foster care, or helping with transportation needs such as repairing cars for single mothers. Each church can survey its community through a community-needs assessment to identify ways their Christ-like stewards might serve outside the church walls.

CHAPTER 4

CHARTING FUTURES

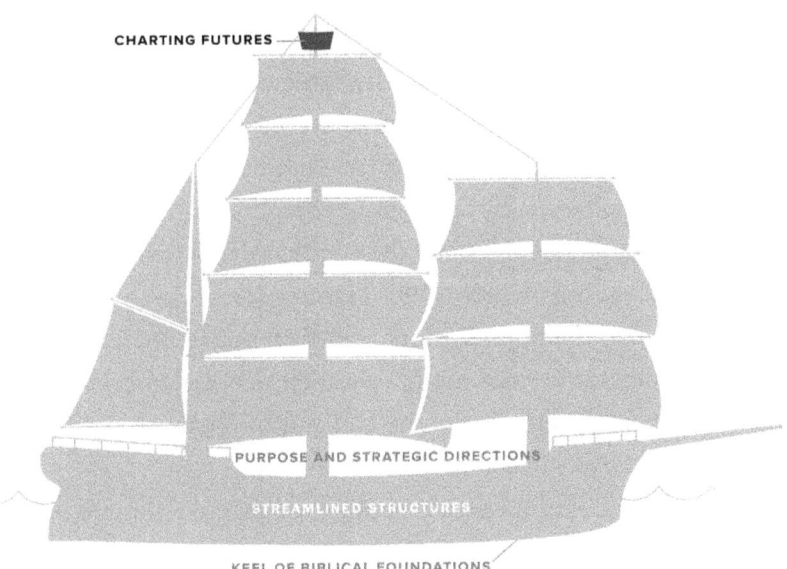

CHARTING FUTURES

PURPOSE AND STRATEGIC DIRECTIONS

STREAMLINED STRUCTURES

KEEL OF BIBLICAL FOUNDATIONS

At the top of an old sailing ship is its "crow's nest." From this position, ancient sailing vessels could see what was out ahead of them. Today, ships, planes, cars, and even hikers use global positioning satellites to guide their journey. But whether one relies on the classic old telescope or the modern dashboard navigation system, knowing what's ahead is critical to one's travels. Knowing the destination informs the journey. Understanding what is out there is important, and it is even more important when it comes to understanding *who* is out there.

I have asked pastors and church leaders, "How does your ministry today differ from your ministry ten years ago?" I am no longer surprised to hear the reply, "Not that much." Many congregations are running the same programs they ran a decade ago, and they do this almost without evaluation—even though their demographic landscape has changed significantly over the years.

Not only are many churches replicating previous years of ministry, many are replicating the ministries of other congregations. I once worked with an older congregation that had five other churches within a few miles of one another, and all of the same denomination. One church had sixty-one people in worship service, one had an attendance of seventy-two, and one had fifty. With each pastor I raised the question whether they had ever thought about merging the churches for greater impact in their area. I suggested they could sell the properties, or maybe give them to an organization like Habitat for Humanity for housing. Perhaps they could set up a seniors' center on one of the larger properties. That way, I suggested, they could join their people to become larger and better together. (Interestingly, the concept of "better together" became the title and subject of a book a decade later.)[3]

Sadly, the idea of a church merger was not on the radar of any of the pastors. In fact, one pastor told me in no uncertain terms he would rather officiate over the death of his church than consider a merger. I was stunned when another responded, "We have a preschool that rents our facility, so I don't need any church members to still draw a paycheck." Churches like this have no future, but churches paying close attention to culture shifts can chart a future and thrive.

---

3   Jim Tomberlin and Warren Bird, *Better Together: Making Church Mergers Work* (San Francisco: Jossey-Bass Books, 2012).

Charting Futures Is More about Exegeting the Culture than Perpetuating a Tradition

While the keel of our church, representing the biblical foundation, is not up for negotiation, program adjustments must be made to connect with issues people face today. Our foundations are the transcultural, essential beliefs and values we embrace. But our ministry offerings, while biblical, must also be culturally relevant to connect with people. Charting the future of a church is all about exegeting (explaining, illuminating, interpreting) the culture. Perhaps ten years ago few saw the need for an eating-disorder support group, but now most understand the need. Maybe a decade ago an AA recovery group was active in the church, but now so is a sexual-brokenness group.

The explosion of technology has handed new ministry opportunities to the church. Web sites beat the old Yellow Pages any day of the week, and a congregation of any size can promote itself attractively and professionally on social media. Databases make tracking membership easy, and congregants are instantly reachable through text messages. In many congregations, online giving has grown to such a degree that they no longer pass offering plates during services.

When charting the future of our churches, we must consider how things have changed in our communities and our world. We must *exegete* the culture. More particularly, we must ask who is out there and how we can best help them experience the reality of Jesus Christ.

Charting Futures Is More about Felt Needs than Assumed Remedies

After years of working with churches and church leadership, I know that too often pastors assume they know what people want from a church. And this is a bad assumption. Of course we all need a relationship with Jesus Christ, but people have personal tastes and preferences about worship, community life, and growth opportunities. Charting futures is more about felt needs than assumed remedies.

Take worship, for example. I once worked with a church that copied their worship service from a Willow Creek style of the 1990s. They thought it was contemporary. I asked why they used that style of music, and the worship pastor responded with, "This is what seekers want." I asked how he knew that. The church was located in an affluent community, and I had an idea that some of their car radios were tuned to classical stations, and for some, jazz. The question was, who was out there? In the final analysis, the worship pastor and the other church leaders had no idea what seekers or anyone else wanted. They were just simply doing what other churches were doing. We should not make assumptions about the kind of music people want or the type of activities they will attend. We need to do our homework. We need to ask them. (As an aside, the number-one style of music listened to in the United States is country, with 52 percent of people having country music preset on their car radios. Yet how many churches use that music style in their churches? We might be surprised how well people respond to an occasional country barbecue, square dance for seniors, or line dancing for singles.) As always, the question is, who is out there?

Another area to consider is community life. Young adults who value community may assume that everyone wants to join a small group. Yet sometimes, when people get in their fifties and have kids and grandkids living nearby, they can feel like they are already in a small group. Furthermore, many people are already engaged in small communities through jobs, sports, hobbies, school, and so on. For some, adding another small-group community can seem too much. At this time in life, many people want a great worship service, a solid message from Scripture, and perhaps a chance to volunteer in a ministry of their interest. They will benefit from Christian support, but that support may not be in the form of a small group.

Charting futures is not about assuming we know what all people want. It is about reaching out to meet perceived and real needs. And it is about understanding that what is going on in people's lives is what informs ministry direction.

Charting Futures Is More about Multiple Venues than One Format

Multiple programming options give people choice. While multiple venues can become more complex and expensive, they certainly connect more people to our churches. Worship is a good example. Most churches with multiple services choose the same style of worship for each service. Megachurches and even some smaller churches seem to prefer this format. But many mid to large size churches find that in their demographic they can reach more people by offering different styles of worship. Rather than forcing people to choose either their church's style of worship, or the worship style of the church down the street, they offer two or three different styles within their own church from which people can choose. They might have a contemporary service for one group, and a traditional service for another.

A second example is small groups. My daughter attends Christ's Church of the Valley in Peoria, Arizona. CCV exceeds twenty-five thousand in worship attendance, and small groups are essential to their ministry. Groups give adults the chance to connect with others like themselves. They can "study the Bible, explore the Christian faith, share life's challenges, or participate in activities in areas of similar interest," according the church's Web site. Growth groups focus on spiritual growth, Bible study, and deepening friendships, whereas connection groups focus on building friendships, sharing common interests, and participating in social activities.

Singles can join a small group just for singles, or they can be involved in a more general small group. While my daughter hangs out with other singles, she is free to join an intergenerational group where singles, families, kids of various ages, and even dogs are connected. CCV's multi venue offers attractive choices for people at various times in their lives.

The multi-venue approach to church life runs counter to the popular "simple church"[4] approach to ministry, where a church intentionally limits its programming, but seeks to do what they do with the highest of quality. Granted, the multi-venue church can implode under the requisite financial and volunteer support needed, but where reasonable, even just a few options can help a church better accomplish its mission.

I have received phone calls from church and lay leaders chairing pastoral-search committees. They want to figure out the process they need to put in place to find a new pastor. I always tell them that, by all means, we can talk about the process. But before talking about the process, I want them to first realize they are in a strategic time for charting their church's future. It is not just a matter of unplugging this and plugging in that. When a church is at a crossroads, as it is when seeking a new pastor, that is the strategic time to evaluate how their community has changed over the last ten years, and how it will look ten years from now. That is huge.

Each of our congregations, whether in pastoral transition or not, are still at a place where we can chart our future. We are not victims, especially when knowing that the desired destination wisely informs our journey.

Hoisting the Sails

Here are some ways a congregation can better chart the future:

---

4   Thom S. Rainer and Eric Geiger, *Simple Church: Returning to God's Process for Making Disciples* (Nashville: B&H Publishing Group, 2006).

GENERATIONAL STUDIES

Articles and books are available that compare and contrast the four generations that make up the American landscape—*Builders, Boomers, Busters,* and *Bridgers.* An example is *One Church, Four Generations.*[5] A good bit of material also speaks to the concerns of Boomers moving into their retirement years and Millennials (Busters) moving into church leadership roles. A church whose leaders study the many available resources can minimize generational tensions within their congregation, as well as identify ways to better minister to each of these four subcommunities.

LIFE-STAGE STUDIES

Similar to generational studies, life-stage studies can provide useful information on the between families, newly married, neoparental, young children, single parenting, first teen, empty nest, and retirement life stages. Seminars, socials, or support groups can connect people within these affinity groups, as well as draw them more into the life of the church as a whole.

PEER FOCUS GROUPS

Conducting focus sessions with life-stage groups is highly instructive. In my Ministry to Adults course, I asked students to conduct focus groups by asking questions such as:

What is life like for you as a parent of young children (or empty nester, etc.)?
What are the highlights or blessings of your current life stage?
What are the challenges or potential crises inherent in your life stage?

---

5   Gary McIntosh, *One Church, Four Generations: Understanding and Reaching All Ages in Your Church* (Grand Rapids: Baker Books, 2002).

How can the congregation as a whole assist you as young marrieds (or retirees, or whatever)?

Interestingly, in addition to a gaining a snapshot of what life looks like for a particular group of people at a particular stage of life, students frequently heard interviewees thank them for listening. For many of them, it was the first time anyone ever asked them for their opinions. It is a sad thing to realize that we as leaders talk more than we listen. We can do better.

Public Schools

Much information on community demographics is available from local school systems. Projected student enrollments, as well as neighborhood trends, are identified for each district's planning purposes.

Community Demographic Reports

Denominations like the Church of the Nazarene or the Presbyterian Church (USA) have research departments that provide community demographics. A church can get free information just by entering their zip code into a menu link, or they can order a fuller report for a nominal cost.[6]

The Percept Group

The Percept Group has relationships with over five hundred denominational organizations, and according to their Web site, they "have amassed the largest and most accurate church location database in existence. We call it ChurchLink and it contains over 100,000 church locations and is updated nearly every day."

Percept offers reliable and innovative demographic resources for any level of church ministry. Of their many reports, there is "First

---

6   http://maps.nazarene.org/DemographicsNazarene/.

View," which provides a powerful introduction to church ministry at a relatively low cost. "Ministry Area Profile" is the highest standard for a complete and detailed community demographic package, and has been used by more than 45,000 churches of all sizes. "Revision" is an optional self-guided process that takes a congregation through a series of visioning and planning exercises to develop a vision statement, mission, and ministry plan.[7]

SPERLING'S BEST PLACES

Sperling's *Best Places* is a Web site created and maintained by author and researcher Bert Sperling. The site "offers information about cities and zip codes in the United States including climate, economy, population, demographics, education, cost of living, and employment."[8]

---

7   www.perceptgroup.com.
8   https://www.bestplaces.net/.

CHAPTER 5

NAVIGATING CHANGE

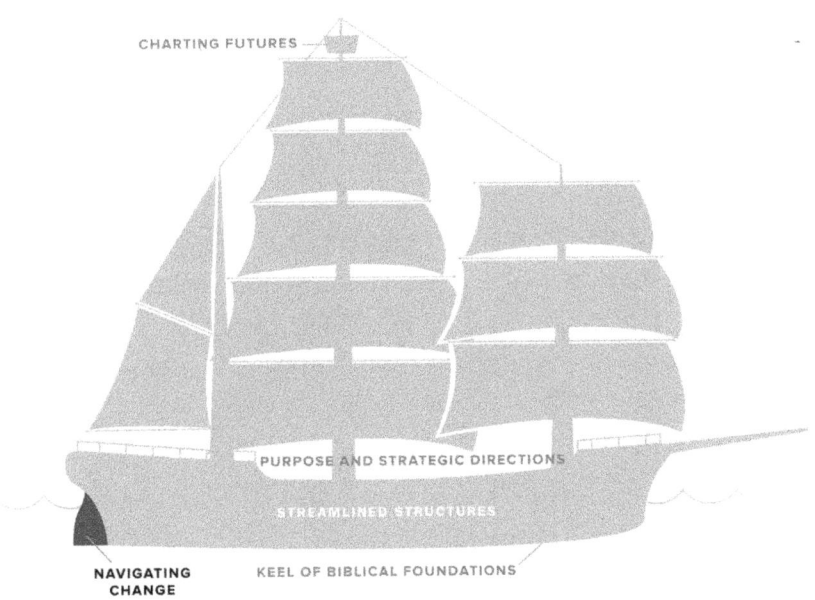

CHARTING FUTURES

PURPOSE AND STRATEGIC DIRECTIONS

STREAMLINED STRUCTURES

NAVIGATING CHANGE　　KEEL OF BIBLICAL FOUNDATIONS

The rudder is an underwater blade used in steering and guiding the direction of a ship. I have emphasized how important it is to know who is out there—in other words, to understand our neighborhood demographics. But if we are not able to steer our ministry in their direction, we really cannot reach them. The ability to navigate change, to change ministry direction, is essential for congregational life.[9] That takes a rudder.

Resistance to change is rather common among churches. The nature of ministry makes managing change especially difficult for local congregations. This is not difficult to understand. First, we have an unchanging message, and sometimes implementing change may appear as if we are tinkering with the message. Second, local churches work with volunteers, and therefore they do not have the authority to insist on change, the way they would if working with staff members. And third, the church is a family; we try hard not to offend anyone, especially the "weaker brother."

Nevertheless, change is inevitable, and resistance to it will paralyze a congregation if it is permitted to do so. A church committed to evangelism and edification of believers must use all means possible to point people to Christ, and then to present them mature in him. While biblical purposes remain unmovable, the means of accomplishing evangelism and discipleship, and other purposes in the church, must remain flexible.

Navigating Change Is More about an Ongoing Process than Crisis Management

Crisis management is sometimes necessary, but navigating a change in ministry direction is more of an ongoing process. One cannot steer a boat that is not moving! Yet when it is moving, even slowly, its course can be guided. Unfortunately, most churches consider moving in a new ministry direction only when their sails are sagging and they have lost all momentum. Consultants too often, unfortunately, are brought in only after something is broken. It is much better to get an occasional

---

9   Some of the material in this chapter is taken from *Solving Church Education's Ten Toughest Problems*, chapter nine, by John R. Cionca. The entire book is available online at: http://www.ministrytransitions.org/Solving-Church-Problems.html.

tune-up than to wait for a complete overhaul. Using the rudder of our ship, making ministry tweaks is easier than making major directional corrections. Navigating change is more about an ongoing process than crisis management.

The more I study congregational life, the more I view change as a process requiring a reasonable amount of time. Usually, a new pastor who makes some changes, even during the honeymoon period, does not upset people. But no congregation wants change to overwhelm them. The final step in implementing change may move swiftly, but the overall process, including planning, ownership, communication, and implementation, needs adequate time.

Not everyone responds to change in the same manner.[10] In every congregation there are innovators, those creative leaders who are way ahead of the pack. At the opposite end there are resisters, who want everything to remain at the status quo. But the majority of the people fall on a continuum somewhere in between. Some are "early adopters" while others are "later adopters," but as a whole, this larger middle group will accept change.

While allowing resisters to express their feelings regarding changes in the church, large investments of personal time with them is rarely productive. Winning the support of legitimizers, however, is critical to the process of navigating change. Legitimatizers are the people a congregation follows. They might be a part of the formal leadership, or they might be a part of the informal structure. Either way, congregants want to know what these respected people think of the proposed change. Convincing a congregation that a change is legitimate is more easily accomplished when respected, key people openly support the move.

---

10   According to Everett M. Rogers in *Diffusion of Innovations* (New York: Free Press, 2001), 2.5% of people are innovators, 13.5% are early adopters, 34% are part of the early majority, 34% are part of the late majority, and 16% are laggards.

Their support is easier to obtain when change is an ongoing process, rather than something required in a crisis moment.

Navigating Change Is More about Problem Solving than Authoritative Answers

Psychologist John B. Watson has demonstrated the reality of "one-trial learning." If you enter a room and sit on the left, the next time you enter the room, you are more likely to sit in that same general location. Over time, these neurological patterns deepen and become embedded. Resistance to change is just not stubbornness, because change can be both psychologically and physiologically distressing to people.

Whether or not a given church practice is the best form for accomplishing a biblical function is irrelevant to people entrenched through habit. To them, the form has meaning because of its association with their worship of God. Therefore, before changes are implemented, wise leaders seek assurance that a new suggestion is the best answer to address a concern.

Using problem-solving techniques minimizes poor changes. Good problem solving moves from identifying possible solutions to selecting the best solution. Involving those affected by anticipated changes, working through a small change group, and using problem-solving techniques will assure a specific change is the best alternative.

Several years ago I worked with a congregation that had a facility that was too big and costly for their size of congregation. They considered four options for addressing their shrinking membership. One was relocating, one was retooling to reach their changing community, one was merger, and the last option was dissolution—selling their assets, distributing the proceeds to missions, and releasing their people to join congregations closer to their homes. Those were their four perceived options, and it was huge that the church board didn't just announce one Sunday, "Hey, we just decided we are going to merge with the church down the street" (or any of the other options). Their people would have been blown away. The board was wiser than that. For a period of time they had ongoing discussions with the congregation regarding their challenge and the possible options for what to do about it. Rather than a few people in a back room deciding the fate of 350 people, they used open problem solving to address their main issue. Navigating change is more about problem solving than authoritative answers.

Navigating Change Is More about Credibility than Blind Trust

It will come as no surprise that people are more willing to follow a leader who has consistently demonstrated integrity. Therefore, establishing credibility among those guiding the congregation is imperative. When pastors or program leaders make sweeping changes too early in a ministry, they have not given the congregation sufficient time to trust them. The people don't know if they are really there to nurture the ministry or if they are just driving a personal agenda. For example, in one town a pastor promised his congregation, "Build a church that will seat a thousand, and I'll pack it out every Sunday." Shortly after the facility was completed, the pastor left. Except for an occasional interdenominational rally, the building is never filled. Each Sunday that congregation enters a visible reminder that pastors cannot be trusted. And a congregation burned by a pastor is slow to welcome the ideas of a new minister.

The admonition against placing a novice in office underscores the importance of credibility. Pastors are better off building trust levels first, then fighting for innovations later. Demonstrating credibility now fosters receptivity for later recommendations. The magnitude of any change is related to the magnitude of the leadership's credibility, and the more unsettling a change (like renaming the church or modifying its constitution), the greater the credibility needed on the part of the leader.

The pastor's affirmation of staff members and elders also builds trust, and this makes a congregation more willing to follow the recommendations of these leaders.

We should not expect church people to blindly trust the church board or the professional staff. Only a demonstrated credibility over time enables us to navigate change. When people believe that their staff and board have their best interest at heart, they are more willing to move with changes.

Almost everyone believes change of one sort or another is important. Modernity has its place. We would rather drive cars than walk to work. We would rather catch the news on the Internet than wait for a messenger to herald the word on foot. And we would rather use indoor plumbing than an outhouse. Change is helpful. While too much change, coming too often, can be challenging, a fixed rudder is detrimental to ministry. Congregations need moveable rudders, capable of guiding ships through rough waters. Pastors are entrusted with the unchanging gospel of reconciliation, and their goal is to present all people mature in Christ. This prioritizes the tasks of evangelism and edification. While these purposes are timeless, changes within our culture continually make possible new ways of accomplishing these tasks with greater relevance.

The question most people ask when a new idea is presented is, "Is this change really necessary?" If a congregation is confident in the credibility of its leadership and understands the reasons behind a proposed change, it will likely offer less resistance to change designed to help the church carry out its purpose.

Hoisting the Sails

Readiness-for-Change Inventories

Church consultants understand the significance of a congregation's willingness to change. Church leaders may say they want changes, but how true is this of the whole congregation? Resources such as Bill Easum's *Complete Ministry Audit* provide instruments to assess a congregation's comfort level with change.[11] Coaching around the change process can then take the church further up and further in.

COMMUNICATING MOTIVES

Congregations are shaped through interaction with the pastoral staff, as well as through responsive communication with all church leadership. Letting people hear what our heart is telling us helps them understand why specific changes are necessary and being suggested. In less formal settings, such as committee meetings, home settings, and luncheons, pastors share their vision for dynamic, relevant ministry, and affirm the church's unchanging purpose—all while communicating motives and encouraging innovative methods.

FOSTERING HEALTHY DISCONTENT

Advertisers recognize that people will not move from one product to another without some identifiable displeasure with their current product. The same is true for changing programs in churches. Showing the limitations of a church program readies people for a better solution. When a sound, new solution is offered, the church is one step closer to accepting it.

ACCEPTING PEOPLE'S FEELINGS

Some leaders make the egregious mistake of squelching opposition, but all communication theorists agree that allowing for differences of opinion is a better long-term strategy for assuring general acceptance of a change. While people's views are challenged by proposed changes, their sense of worth is devalued when they are not allowed to voice disagreement and displeasure. Patrick Lencioni believes that "people

---

11   Bill Easum, *The Complete Ministry Audit* (Nashville: Abingdon Press, 2006).

do not innately have the need to be right; they have the need to be heard."[12] People's feelings are real to them, and wise leaders recognize the legitimacy of one's thoughts and sensations, even if they present an opposing viewpoint. Giving thanks for what a current program has accomplished in the past while sharing a vision of what the new program could do in the future wins more allegiance than outright rejection of a difference of opinion.

Associating Changes with Accepted Values

When the leaders of one church I consulted wanted to change versions of the pew Bible, they promoted the importance of using a modern translation that both members and guests could understand. "We want people seeking Christ to be able to follow along as the Word of God is taught," said the senior pastor. While some church members were unhappy with the suggested change, the transition was relatively smooth because it was linked to the higher value of more people being able to clearly understand Scripture.

Using a Small Change Team

Not everybody affected by a change should be part of the change process. Working through a change team of five to seven people is very effective, depending, of course, on the nature of the proposed change. The key leaders related to an issue are best able to strategize, communicate, and implement change. And the coordination and promotion are best accomplished through a representative smaller group. While the adoption of a major change, such as relocation, may require the approval of the whole congregation, using a smaller change team to study, promote, and bring the recommendation is always beneficial.

---

12   Patrick Lencioni, "The Five Dysfunctions of a Team." Presentation given at the Willow Creek Summit, 2003.

CHAPTER 6

CORPORATE PRAYER

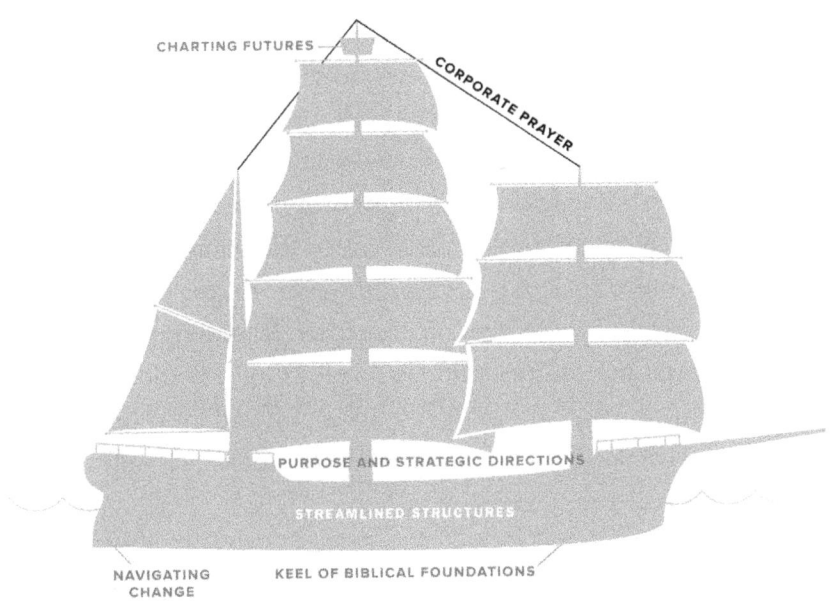

CHARTING FUTURES

CORPORATE PRAYER

PURPOSE AND STRATEGIC DIRECTIONS

STREAMLINED STRUCTURES

NAVIGATING CHANGE

KEEL OF BIBLICAL FOUNDATIONS

We have been exploring the structural integrity of ministry by using the model of a ship for illustrative purposes. Setting a course for church health demands a structural integrity built on the interdependency of biblical foundations (the ship's keel), purposeful and strategic direction (the bridge), the charting of futures (the crow's nest), and navigational change (the rudder). The final part of the structural integrity of ministry is Corporate Prayer—represented by the rigging of a ship, which takes the force of the wind and propels the ship forward in the water.

Prayer is a spiritual discipline essential for eternal life, according to the apostle Paul: "Everyone who calls on the name of the Lord will be saved" (Rom. 10:13). The apostle John tells us prayer is also essential for fellowship with God: "If we confess our sins, he is faithful and just and will forgive us our sins and purify us from all unrighteousness" (1 John 1:9). Prayer is essential for many other things, including effective witness, resisting temptation, and daily guidance: "Ask the Lord of the harvest, therefore, to send out workers into his harvest field" (Matt. 9:38); "Watch and pray so that you will not fall into temptation. The spirit is willing, but the flesh is weak" (Mark 14:38); and, "Trust in the Lord with all your heart and lean not on your own understanding; in all your ways submit to him, and he will make your paths straight" (Prov. 3:5–6).

Prayer is more than all of that, however. Prayer is the corporate rigging that ties the whole structure together. It undergirds the pastoral staff, is essential to volunteerism, and seeks God for more workers to move into the harvest. Corporate prayers are offered for transformation, sound decision-making, and for all necessary resources—all the things essential for effective congregational life.

Corporate Prayer Is More about Daily Dialogues than Campus Events

Prayer is about Christ followers in our churches keeping an ongoing dialogue with God. Certainly prayer can be a onetime event in the church building, but it is more about praying continually, as the Bible tells us—praying without ceasing.[13]

My mother talked to God regularly—I mean out loud, throughout the whole day. When she finished gardening, she would say, "Thanks,

---

13   First Thessalonians 5:16–18: "Rejoice always, pray continually, give thanks in all circumstances; for this is God's will for you in Christ Jesus."

Jesus. That was good." After cleaning windows, I would hear, "Okay, Lord, we've got that taken care of. What's next?" As a little guy, I was constantly looking around and wondering, "Where's Jesus?" Mom had an ongoing, oral conversation with Jesus throughout the day, and at its best, that is what prayer is. Several of God's children interceding together at the church and talking to their Father is very important. But prayer is a spiritual discipline, the corporate rigging tying the Christian life together when Christ followers are daily talking with their Lord.

Corporate Prayer Is More about Adoration than Intercession

We frequently use the word *pray* for the word *ask*. Who has not heard a prayer something like, "Lord, I pray you would be with us today"? What we are really saying is, "Lord, I ask that you would be with us today." Too often, prayer, which is a petition to God, has become synonymous with requesting information or asking for something. Yet prayer is about intercession, confession, adoration, and thanksgiving.

At the end of a service, a pastor invited, "And all God's people said?" While most of the members parroted "Amen," one little boy bellowed, "Gimme!" He missed it, but his observation was not far from the practice of most people. Too much of our prayer is "gimme gimme." Asking is good. In fact, God commands us to do so.[14] But basking in the wonder of God, and glorifying him through adoration and thanksgiving is better.

Corporate Prayer Is More about Submission than Petition

Authentic prayer is more about aligning ourselves with God's values than asking God to do something outside the box in our lives. Certainly Philippians 4:6–7 assures us we can pray about anything that makes

---

14 "Ask and it will be given to you; seek and you will find; knock and the door will be opened to you" (Matt. 7:7); "Do not be anxious about anything, but in every situation, by prayer and petition, with thanksgiving, present your requests to God. And the peace of God, which transcends all understanding, will guard your hearts and your minds in Christ Jesus" (Phil. 4:6–7).

us anxious. We ought to bring these things to God, but prayer is more about submission than petition.

If I entreat, "Lord, help me reach my neighbor for Christ; help me to have an opportunity to talk with him about Jesus," is it likely God wants me to do that? Of course. Charles Finney made this observation about prayer in the fourth of his *Revival Lectures*: "But prayer produces such a change in us as renders it consistent for God to do as it would not be consistent for Him to do otherwise." In other words, prayer is aligning our desires with God's desire.

Consider Jonah and the city of Nineveh. Did God really change his mind about his response to the behavior of these Assyrian people? Not really. Think about why God sent Jonah to the Ninevites in the first place. He wanted them to turn from their wicked ways and repent. God wanted them to adopt his own desire for their lives. Likewise, our praying is really coming alongside God's purpose for our lives.

The term "Christian" can be problematic sometimes because it means too many different things in too many different contexts. The term "Christ follower" is one I like to use because it implies movement. If I am just stationary, or walking away from God's will, I am not a very good Christ follower. What should a Christian's life look like? It should be one that values more and more what God values. Therefore, prayer is more about the submission of our lives than the petitions of our mouths.

Corporate prayer—God's children in conversation with the Father about the body of Christ—is essential to the health of the congregation. God's Word is clear that "The prayer of a righteous person is powerful and effective."[15] Strategizing or doing ministry in our own strength is futile. Aligning ourselves with God's leading, however, will produce a successful voyage.

---

15   James 5:16: "Therefore confess your sins to each other and pray for each other so that you may be healed. The prayer of a righteous person is powerful and effective."

Hoisting the Sails

TEAM MEETING PRAYER

Most boards and ministry teams with which I am familiar open their meetings with prayer. Usually, team meeting prayers acknowledge that the members are God's servants and they want his will in their deliberations. It is my observation that prayers at these team meetings are usually quite brief, and I encourage churches to extend these prayer times. When I became the pastor of one congregation, I was amazed at how long elder-board meetings ran. Three to four hours per meeting was not unusual. When we began the practice of praying for the first half hour of our monthly meetings, including interceding for ten church families at each meeting, the length of our evenings surprisingly began to shrink. Eventually we were able to accomplish each month's agenda, along with extended prayers, in an hour and a half.

PERSONAL PRAYER JOURNALS

Many of my friends maintain prayer logs. For years they have entered praises and prayer requests on these records. While "arrow prayers" (those spontaneous words of praise or intercessions) are great, "journal prayers" are equally valuable—particularly for prevailing prayer. One of my friends, for example, has me on his Thursday list, remembering me each week before the Father.

PHYSICAL REMINDERS

Some people carry with them a personal reminder of their relationship with Christ. One of my friends wears a cross on a chain, and another carries a small aluminum cross in his pocket. Another carries a nail in his pocket to remember the sacrifice of Christ on our behalf, while another carries a small "David stone" in his pocket to remember what God can accomplish through one who is willing. When an eye sees or a hand touches the object, one remembers to talk with the Lord.

CONVERSATIONAL PRAYER

Conversational prayer was introduced to American evangelicals in 1973 by Rosalind Rinker in her book, *Prayer: Conversing with God.* She defined prayer as "a dialogue between two persons who love each other." Conversational prayer is one conversation between a prayer group and God. Instead of people individually speaking their own, often longer prayers, all the participants join in with brief offerings on a same theme. When that concern seems exhausted, a new area is prayed over, again all giving short prayers around that theme. It is just like a conversation around a table, with full interaction on a subject before moving on to another subject.

ONE-BREATH PRAYERS

I have participated in prayer times when the ground rule was that prayers could only be one breath long. With a format like this, obviously more concerns are covered. But perhaps more importantly, young Christ followers feel free to join in. Under normal circumstances, younger Christians (both by spiritual age and chronological age) would be reticent to vocalize a prayer, especially if they had to follow a godly saint who prayed eloquently for every church and world concern. But everyone can offer a prayer of one breath.

SMALL GROUPS

A great place for corporate prayer is in small-group settings. In fact, if a group has more than eight participants, it should probably be subdivided in order to make people feel more comfortable vocalizing a prayer. Some small-group Bible studies open with a prayer, and then later they break down into smaller groups for deeper praise and intercession.

Men's Groups

It is no secret that men are often uncomfortable with outward demonstrations of spirituality. For insight on this, I suggest reading *Why Men Hate Going to Church*.[16] I used to lead a couples group where two men rarely contributed, and they never prayed out loud. A year later, when these same men were in a men's group I led, they both entered the discussions and even participated in open prayer. Why were they uncomfortable in mixed groups? Some have suggested that men don't want to look stupid in front of their wives. Perhaps more importantly, they don't want to look stupid in front of other men's wives! The point is that men's triads or small groups are another great place for conversations with God.

Just Do It!

I have taught classes on prayer, but I have always wondered if people were praying more as a result of those classes. When I was in the pastorate, there was a time when I determined I would no longer talk about prayer, but I would simply pray on all occasions. After meeting with people, I would say, "Before you go, let's have a word of prayer." Before a class or a rehearsal, I would suggest, "Let's pause for a moment and offer this time to God." I am convinced that prayer is more caught than taught. My advice is to talk less about prayer and just do it.

---

16   David Murrow, *Why Men Hate Going to Church* (Nashville: Thomas Nelson Publishers, 2005).

PART TWO

EFFECTIVE LEADERSHIP

CHAPTER 7

MOBILIZED VOLUNTEERS

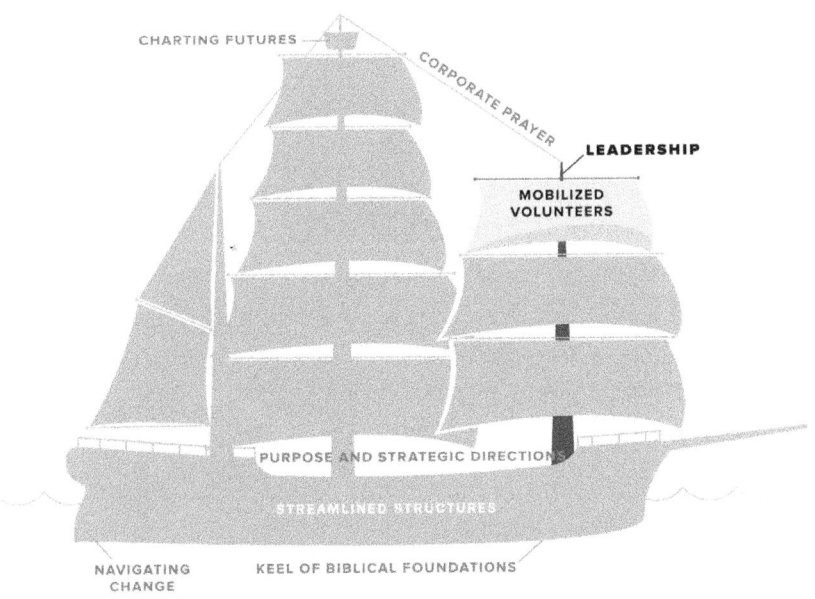

The next part of the ship we will examine is the *Mast of Leadership*. On this mast are three sails—representing those who serve and give guidance to the church's ministry. The sail of Mobilized Volunteers describes the type of effectiveness needed by those who contribute their time and talents to accomplish the church's ministry. The sail of Engaged Lay Ministers describes the deeper level of commitment made by a special group of non-paid staff, those willing to take ownership of a particular task. And the sail of Competent Pastors analyzes the role of those who are remunerated for their service.

Let's begin by looking at Mobilized Volunteers, and the need for all on board jumping in and giving a hand to the work of the ministry.

A number of images are used in the New Testament to describe the church. Perhaps the two best-known analogies are the temple and the body. As for the temple, all those who come to Christ become living stones. The apostle Peter wrote, "You also, like living stones, are being built into a spiritual house to be a holy priesthood, offering spiritual sacrifices acceptable to God through Jesus Christ" (1 Pet. 2:5). While believers maintain their individual identities, together they become Christ's living temple. All the bricks are important, but the structure is incomplete if they remain on pallets lying on the ground.

The church is also called the body of Christ. The apostle Paul said, "Just as a body, though one, has many parts, but all its many parts form one body, so it is with Christ. For we were all baptized by one Spirit so as to form one body—whether Jews or Gentiles, slave or free—and we were all given the one Spirit to drink. Even so the body is not made up of one part but of many" (1 Cor. 12:12–14). Jesus himself is the head of the body: "He is the head of the body, the church; he is the beginning and the firstborn from among the dead, so that in everything he might have the supremacy" (Col. 1:18). In our physical bodies, all body parts contribute to the wellness and function of the whole body. Similarly, in the body of Christ, each Christian's involvement is required for the church's structural integrity and wellness.

If 100 percent of the people in a faith community are using their spiritual giftedness to serve others, their sail is all the way up, and they are catching the maximum wind of the Spirit. If only half the people are involved in impacting other lives, the sail is only half unfurled. Healthy congregations maximize member ministries in order to raise Christ's banner high. Because every Christian is a minister, our expectations for volunteerism should be high.

Volunteer Service Is More about Teams than Individual Performers

In the world of sports, every team would like to have a few superstars. They are the outstanding performers who dazzle the crowd. But less notable players who are just as significant are the impact players. Impact players may not excite the crowd, but they consistently step up to do whatever is needed for victory. Many teams, even with their superstar and impact players, fail to go the distance during the playoff season. They have all the necessary raw talent, but they lack requisite teamwork. Teams that win championships maximize the skill level of each player through the synergy of teamwork.

Whatever ministries a church offers, they can be maximized through volunteers serving together. Needs are too great and opportunities too plentiful for any individual to fulfill them all. Team ministry has many advantages over individual service, and some of these are:

Complementary giftedness

Spreading the weight of ministry on several shoulders

A natural encouragement and support network

Ministry recipients can identify with different role models

Absenteeism can be covered more naturally

Skill development is maximized across the team

Safety risks and false accusations are better safeguarded

Team interaction can model the very concepts a team is presenting

Volunteer Service Is More about Retention than Recruitment

For eighteen years I conducted surveys of church discipleship concerns, particularly their challenges. When results are tabulated from across the congregations, the issue that has always drawn the most attention is volunteer recruitment. Regardless of congregational size, location, theology, or church governance, all churches express a concern with finding enough volunteers to run their programs.

Generational differences impact volunteerism. Builders indicate they primarily serve out of duty (loyalty to the church means that I will serve). Boomers primarily serve out of obligation (since my children are in the program, I probably should take a turn staffing some of the sessions). Busters and Millennials say they serve primarily out of interest (this ministry is exactly what I've been looking for).

Economic differences also impact volunteerism. In my surveys, I have found that the more affluent the constituency, the more accustomed they are to buying services rather than volunteering. On the other hand, people who care for their own lawns, car, babysitting, and tax returns also expect to pitch in and care for their church.

Despite these differences, however, most churches misunderstand their staffing shortfalls. The challenge facing these congregations is not primarily that they can't find enough volunteers. The truth is that many churches cannot retain those who have tried volunteer service. The coin of staffing, then, has two sides—recruitment and retention. While church surveys reveal that most leaders think they have a recruitment problem, what they really have is a retention problem.

If everyone who served as a volunteer this past year returned to serve again next year (and for the next ten years, for that matter), then churches would not have to look for new volunteers. Volunteer service is more about retention than recruitment. Growing churches would only need additional volunteers to serve their expanding ministry.

Customer service experts tell us it takes ten times more work to find a new customer than to keep an old one. Translated into the church setting, this means it is much harder to find a new volunteer than it is to keep a member already happily serving.

Volunteer turnover is understandable, if for no other reason than people discover other service options they would like to try. Yet volunteer turnover can be minimized by carefully matching a person's ministry gifts with service setting, and then providing training and encouragement so that their service is rewarding. Closing the back door where volunteers exit is far easier than adding new front doors. Service to the church is more than simply filling a ministry slot. We must encourage people to employ their giftedness over the long haul for kingdom impact.

Volunteer Service Is More about Invitation than Coercion

Some years ago I compiled and edited a book I entitled *Inviting Volunteers to Minister.*[17] I did not call the book *Recruiting Volunteers*. For one thing, many people see the word *recruitment* as negative. Besides militaristic associations, it also connotes being drawn into something, perhaps even against one's own will. A program manager whose focus is the number of ministry slots that need filling may be tempted to pressure people into volunteering. But asking those to serve because no one else will do it is a lose-lose-lose proposition. The program recipients lose because they have a leader who really does not want to be there. The volunteer loses because they do not have any joy in their service. And the program coordinator loses because the dropout rate among coerced workers is high.

On the other hand, a program director with a more helpful attitude (the attitude of "Let me help you become all that God wants you to be") will enjoy a fruitful solicitation process. This type of leader realizes that God's plan for spiritual growth is the sharing of personal gifts and talents. In other words, fulfillment and joy are by-products of service. Therefore, when I invite somebody to consider a ministry opportunity, I am actually doing that person a favor—rather than stopping up the

---

17   John R. Cionca, *Inviting Volunteers to Minister* (Colorado Springs: Standard Publishing/David C. Cook, 1999).

hole in a staffing dike. I am helping people fulfill their creation design. That is why volunteer service is more about invitation than coercion.

Volunteer Service Is More about Passions than Programs

There are many reasons why people don't volunteer. A time crunch hinders many. Some simply do not understand the benefits of service to the church. Others have been burnt-out in a previous volunteer ministry. Pointedly, some people just haven't been asked. One reason why people do not serve is that the opportunities presented simply do not include areas of personal interest. They may not enjoy working with children, so why volunteer to work in that area? They might not be musically inclined, so asking them to volunteer in some aspect of the music ministry would not be enticing. And yet in many churches, 75 percent of ministry openings are in these two areas.

Every church has a core program that must be staffed. Filling those ministry positions with people who have a passion for a particular type of service is essential. Unfortunately, the core program in many churches has become too large, outstretching their human resources. They seem always to be behind the staffing curve. When a church is more selective on the activities it schedules, however, it can release people into service areas beyond the core program.

I encourage churches to delineate clearly the ministries they offer, with ministry descriptions for each volunteer position and a small bio of the volunteer filling the position. Unfortunately, many congregations are not effective at showcasing all that is offered in the church, as well as the experiences and talents of their people fulfilling the ministry. The reason for this is that they do not know their people. Service flourishes when individuals can fulfill their creation design in focused ministry opportunities, but volunteerism is hamstrung when church leaders do not know their people.

Another thing I encourage churches to do is view their volunteers not as prospective program workers, but as entrepreneurial servants. We each have unique talents, gifts, and ministries.

Therefore, we should examine our DEPTH: **D**esires, **E**xperiences, **P**ersonality, **T**alents, and the **H**oly Spirit's enabling to discover how we can best fit into the many volunteer service options before us. Even two teachers working together in the same high school class will differ in approach and outlook. One may be an introvert, while the other an extrovert. They come from different backgrounds, and they have different training, life experiences, skills, and passions. Where a person fits best in the mix of things is determined by who they are and where their interests lie. Effective volunteer service is entrepreneurial and more about people's passions than program needs.

Volunteer Service Is More about Experimentation than Speculation

A solid ministry match between who we are by virtue of God's ingenious engineering and what our passions are capitalizes on our whole creation design. Service out of sync with our God-wiring is draining, but service simply living out who we truly are is deeply satisfying.

Many churches are doing a good job at matching volunteers to ministry opportunities. They even conduct classes to help people understand how their unique personalities, abilities, and spiritual gifting can be brought to bear on volunteer opportunities in the church. These types of pre-service self-awareness classes are extremely helpful in minimizing the mismatch when square people are placed into oval ministries. Still, many people need to try a particular ministry for a while to see if they click with it. While it is important to minimize poor ministry matches, at the same time we need to create a service environment where people are encouraged to experiment with various service opportunities. Like doctors fulfilling their rotational internships, several ministry opportunities should be experienced. Over the course of time, specific areas of service will surface that produce inner joy for the volunteer, usually validated by external confirmation from those who observe their effectiveness.

In summary, our goal in volunteerism is for 100 percent of our people to serve the Kingdom in one way or another. This "every member a minister" value is critical for staffing key programs, but it is even more important for the volunteers themselves in fulfilling their creation design.

Hoisting the Sails

Churches can expand their volunteer ministries in a number of ways. Some of those ways follow.

Discovering Seminars on Our Creation Design

Many people who are interested in learning more about themselves come to greater self-awareness about their learning choices, the activities in which they like to engage, and the responsibilities they accept through seminars and classes on our creation design. Insight on personal style, giftedness, motivational wiring, and interactive patterns can positively impact volunteer service. Churches offering classes with resources such as LifeKeys,[18] Network,[19] or similar discovery-type materials, provide a valuable developmental resource to their congregations.

---

18   Jane Kise, David Stark, and Sandra Krebs Hirsh, *Life Keys Discovery Notebook: Discover Who You Are* (Minneapolis: Bethany House Publishers, 2005).
19   Bruce Bugbee, *Network: What You Do Best in the Body of Christ* (Grand Rapids: Zondervan/Willow Creek, 2005).

Short-Term Ministry Opportunities

People today generally are slow to make long-term commitments. Since fewer people are eager to sign up for a one-year ministry assignment, many churches use flexible scheduling to allow people to test the waters of volunteerism. When people learn how enjoyable it is to use their spiritual gifts, they are more willing to sign up for a full season of service. Often, the key to long-term engagement is the short-term opportunity for sampling service.

Director of Volunteer Ministries

Many churches have added to the professional staff a coordinator responsible for volunteerism. This director of volunteer ministries serves to coordinate the personal giftedness of congregants with the various ministry opportunities available. The director also maintains the database of a congregant's volunteer experience and interest, disseminating this information to other members of the church staff and other program coordinators. The director coordinates the process of soliciting volunteers and overseeing their progress.

Faith Stories of Volunteers

People learn by example. Hearing the stories of others who have tried a ministry opportunity and found joy in it is highly motivational. Over time, people in the pews begin realizing that ordinary people just like them have stepped up to serve the church. If they can, why not me? They may not volunteer until personally asked, but they are more likely to accept an invitation to ministry if they have heard the stories of other volunteers.

Pastoral Examples of Volunteer Service

In a healthy congregation, people touch other lives on a consistent basis. Relating some of these personal stories from the pulpit can be highly motivational. Without embarrassing an individual, the pastor can relate the impact a member has had on another person's life. Many great things happen each week through the ministry of the laity, and highlighting some of them for the church family to see reinforces the priority of personal service.

Parade of Children

The average church member has no idea how many volunteers it takes to run their ministry, and that is especially true when it comes to the children's ministry. In many congregations, since the children are in their own program, the adults rarely see all of the children at the same time. To paint a visual image of how many children are being ministered to on a weekly basis, some leaders schedule a children's walk or parade through the sanctuary. The stream of children impacts many in the pews with the number of volunteers needed to touch these young lives for Christ.

Children's Month

Many congregations realize that their children's ministry, more than other ministries, requires a disproportionately large number of volunteers to run a successful program. They also know that the good things happening in the children's work is usually not seen by the adult community. To make sure the congregation knows what is happening with ministry among the children, churches use the month of May to highlight children's ministry. During this month there is usually an added emphasis on volunteer solicitation for the next fall's program. Other things can heighten congregational awareness during children's month, including pastoral affirmation, bulletin inserts, testimonials, banners, and special information and sign-up cards in each row of the sanctuary.

PREACHING ON KINGDOM INVESTMENT

When I ask people what their most valuable commodity is, they usually rank time ahead of money. It makes sense, therefore, to help people more carefully plan their time investments, particularly their time contributions in kingdom activities. Preaching from pertinent Bible passages reveals God's design for Christian service—passages, for example, such as Mark 10:45 (Jesus came not to be served but to serve), 1 Corinthians 12 (the beauty and necessity of complimentary giftedness), 2 Corinthians 5:15 and following (Christ died for us so we would no longer live for ourselves, but live in service as ministers of reconciliation), and Ephesians 2:10 (God has already prepared us for good works of service). Believers fulfill their creation design when complementing and serving one another.

NEW-MEMBER INTERVIEWS

Part of joining a church should be the willingness to participate on a ministry team if at all possible. That is why many congregations use their membership classes to highlight their philosophy of volunteerism and solicit commitments to serve. Some churches use a membership application that features volunteer ministry opportunities on the reverse side. The implication is clear to all who join that every member is a minister.

TEAM MINISTRIES

Research studies reveal that affiliation is a powerful motivator for service. While many people hesitate accepting a responsibility resting solely upon themselves, they are open to trying a ministry shared by a team. Therefore, rather than trying to recruit a volunteer to an individual service task, why not invite them to join a team working together? This relational component adds value through the complementary giftedness of team members, and it also provides a sense of community and camaraderie to the group members.

Operation Andrew

The first thing the apostle Andrew did when he learned about Jesus was to invite his brother, Peter, to meet the Messiah. "Andrew, Simon Peter's brother, was one of the two who heard what John had said and who had followed Jesus. The first thing Andrew did was to find his brother Simon and tell him, 'We have found the Messiah' (that is, the Christ). And he brought him to Jesus" (John 1:40–42). Some churches practice a more decentralized approach to inviting volunteers to minister. While program directors or coordinators conduct final interviews and make official appointments, it is the volunteers in the trenches—the Andrews—who are on the lookout for people to join their various teams. Recruitment to ministry is everyone's business.

CHAPTER 8

ENGAGED LAY
MINISTERS

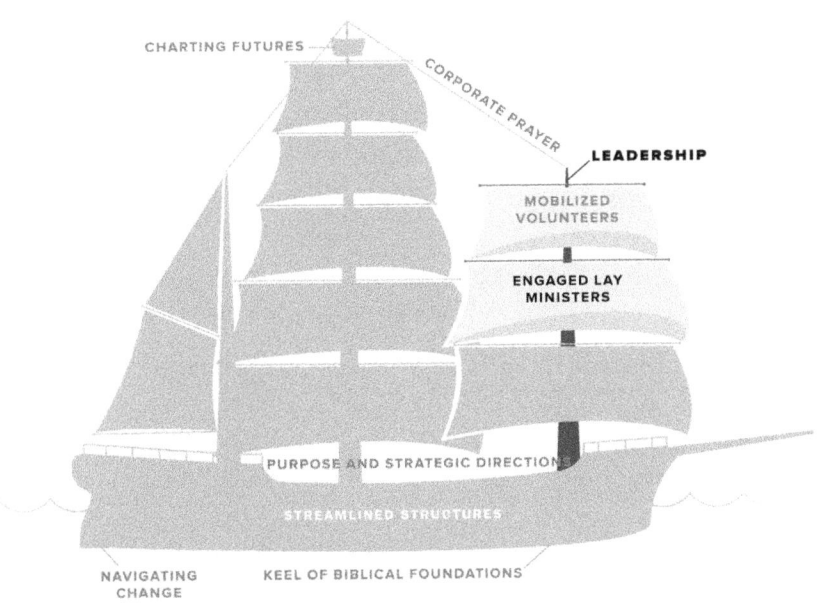

The second sail on the mast of effective leadership is Engaged Lay Ministers. Those supervising volunteer service quickly recognize the different levels of commitment among those who contribute. Unfortunately, some volunteers are "guilted" into service. Others feel like they have to serve, perhaps because their kids are part of the children's ministry and they feel like they should take their turn working with the kiddos. Some serve monthly, maybe ushering during the worship service, or serving in committee work. Some serve weekly and support a critical area of ministry. The more regularly and consistently a volunteer serves, the deeper is the level of their commitment. Engaged lay ministers move from duty to delight, because the way they see it, they are not merely filling a ministry slot. They are touching lives.

Volunteers not serving on a weekly basis might be missing out on a whole new scale of kingdom service. All congregations have individuals with the expertise and available time to assume responsibility for a particular area of ministry on a part-time, or even full-time, volunteer basis. They can make a staff-level commitment, though in reality they are volunteers. Engaged lay ministers are not remunerated for service, but they are as responsible for a ministry area as are the professional church staff.

Engaged Lay Ministry Is More about Ownership than Obligation

In the ship model we have been using, "engaged lay ministers" describes the highest level of volunteer service. The term "minister" is appropriate because of the servant's expertise, passion, and time commitment in accepting responsibility for a critical aspect of congregational life. They typically don't need much supervision. Some of these lay ministers work in congregational care, some in church operations, and others work on the church building itself. Let me provide some examples of engaged lay ministers at work.

The campus at Edinbrook Church is so attractive that their city gave the woman caring for the grounds an award in recognition of her horticultural work. Cindy spends many days each week between Easter and Thanksgiving making Edinbrook a God-honoring, welcoming presence in the community. This kind of presence can prove to be very important. A well-known pastor once said this about his own church campus: "We have a beautiful, well-manicured facility. In fact, I remember one couple visited, came to Christ, and later said, 'We thought if you took care of flowers, you probably cared about people.'"[20] At Edinbrook, Cindy isn't paid to plant flowers, trim shrubs, and nurture the campus. She volunteers. Yet her level of commitment demonstrates how seriously she accepts ownership of that area of ministry.

For years, Trinity Church was blessed by a couple who had accepted responsibility for the church's financial records. The Books (honestly, that was their name) kept the books. While most congregations pay for this kind of work, Trinity was able to allocate their resources to other staff positions because the Books accepted ownership for this dimension of ministry.

John serves Medina Church as a deacon who spends a good deal of time in visitation. Even though Medina has its share of elderly members, the church does not feel it needs a seniors' pastor because John fills that role. He does more than fill it—he owns it. When the church pastor was called to a new church, John's gifts were used in an even wider way when he jumped in with other pastoral functions during the transition.

Jim served Cornerstone Church by keeping the grass on their twelve-acre campus looking great. Their property includes two baseball fields and additional open green spaces. The church owns a professional-grade lawn mower that really moves. Each week, Jim flew across the lawn trying to break his previous speed records. For years, he faithfully cared for the church's grounds, until one day he was invited to join the church staff to oversee the entire physical plant. Jim reminds me of the biblical principle that "Whoever can be trusted with very little can also be trusted with much." (Luke 16:10).

---

20   John MacArthur in *Leadership Journal* (Fall 1991).

These examples show that engaged lay ministry leadership is more about ownership than obligation.

Engaged Lay Ministry Is More about Significant Time than Occasional Service

To accept responsibility for an area of congregational life at the level described above takes expertise, passion, and time. Time, in fact, is what distinguishes engaged lay ministers from other equally committed volunteers. All may be gifted. All may have fervor for a particular area of service. But effective ownership of a ministry is possible only for those who have the requisite time availability.

Duncan has a heart for lost people. He leads Bible studies and volunteers in other capacities, but his passion really is for evangelism. After taking early retirement from a pharmaceutical company, he offered his expanded availability to his church. His pastor gladly let him run with the outreach ministry. Duncan worked full-time as a volunteer, training and leading teams of others to reach their community in the Phoenix area. He had a title and an office, but he didn't spend much time there; he wanted to be out among those who needed to hear the gospel.

Barbara serves Southwood Church in an administrative-assistant position. She and her husband Tom love their congregation, and they both regularly serve their church in significant ways. They raised three sons there. When their youngest son was high school age, Barbara, who was a stay-at-home mom, deepened her service. While the church office has two full-time, paid assistants on staff, on any given day there are three sets of hands covering the operations at Southwood. Barbara is a deeply engaged lay minister.

Five couples at Salem Church, all seniors, meet early on Monday mornings to have coffee, pastries, and exercise. Their exercise of choice is cleaning the church after Sunday activities. They empty all trashcans and refit each with a new liner. They clean all the bathrooms. And they move tables and fold chairs in the classrooms, in preparation for vacuuming. Salem Church has a full-time custodian, but with the size of their church campus, additional paid help would be needed without the consistent work of this volunteer team. They are good examples of engaged lay ministers who faithfully commit to take on an important responsibility over the long haul.

Engaged Lay Ministry Is More about Leaving a Legacy than Marking Time

People who are willing to give their church a chunk of time each week are not likely serving out of guilt or simply trying to fill a ministry slot. They want to make a significant contribution. They have done many nominal things in their lives, and they have also accomplished some great things. But now they want to focus more on doing things that count for eternity. In the words of Bob Buford—they want to move "from success to significance."[21]

Ron and Jim tag team the repairs at Bethel Church. Their aging facility always needs lights replaced, filters changed, locks reset, toilets repaired, pipes flushed, carpets cleaned, and items installed or removed. While they work on an "as needed" basis, they always seem to be there repairing one thing or another. They have done this for years. Considering the cost of calling a professional handyman for just a single repair, these two engaged lay ministers have saved the church thousands of dollars. They do not volunteer because they are bored. Both of them have families and stay very active. Rather, they accept this responsibility because they love the Lord and because they want to use their talents and time for his glory.

When John and his brother sold their financial business, John was in his fifties. He still had a lot of energy, and now that he had more

---

21   Bob Buford, *Halftime: Moving from Success to Significance* (Grand Rapids: Zondervan Publishing House, 2008).

discretionary time than ever, he volunteered to oversee the business operations of his church, including its finances. While John had an office at the church, a title, and worked four days a week, he never took a salary. He didn't need the money, but he did need to steward his gifts and help his church reach the people of their community. Like many others, John does not serve the church out of obligation, but out of a deep desire to "store up for yourselves treasures in heaven."[22]

Unfortunately, too few churches know the blessing and value of lay leaders accepting responsibility for major areas of ministry. Engaged lay ministers serve their church in many different ways. Some I have known have accepted responsibility as videographers, graphic artists, grounds keepers, sound technicians, cooks, webmasters, concierges, grief counselors, and worship leaders. Effective ministry in the future will capitalize on these committed servants and help them make significant contributions for eternity.

Hoisting the Sails

Personal and Leadership Profiles

Most churches use personal and leadership assessments in their hiring process with pastoral and other professional staff. It is also a good practice to provide leadership assessments for key lay leaders. Profiles such as the *DiSC*,[23] *Situational Leadership*,[24] and *StrengthsFinder*[25] can help when considering if people are a good ministry fit for particular areas of church service.

---

22   "But store up for yourselves treasures in heaven, where moths and vermin do not destroy, and where thieves do not break in and steal" (Matt. 6:20).
23   https://www.onlinediscprofile.com/what-is-the-disc-profile/.
24   http://leadership.kenblanchard.com/Situational-Leadership.
25   http://www.strengthsfinder.com/home.aspx.

Personal Invitations

When I was a child, I wanted to build a kite from some materials in my grandfather's workshop. My grandmother encouraged me. She said, "Johnny, just ask. The worst that can happen is that Grampa will say no, so what have you lost? Then again he might say yes, and you'll have your kite." In a study of six hundred teachers from 220 Churches of Christ, only a small percentage said they served in the church because "no one else would do it." The greatest number of respondents volunteered that they were active "because I was asked!"

Pastors must not be afraid to ask for serious commitment from qualified lay leaders who may be able to take ownership of a given ministry. In fact, painting a picture of the blessings and rewards of engaged lay ministry is a big part of the pastoral calling.[26]

Ministry Descriptions

I tell pastors I work with, "Let's recruit with class." Since volunteers freely give of their time, pastors must be respectful when inviting them to service. Respect is communicated through an intentional approach, not in an overly casual manner like, "By the way, when you have some time, let's talk about. . . ." We need to make clear we are asking them to consider the job because of the competencies and commitment we see in them. To help volunteers pray wisely about accepting any new role, we should provide ministry descriptions that delineate the specific responsibilities of each position.

---

26 "So Christ himself gave the apostles, the prophets, the evangelists, the pastors and teachers, to equip his people for works of service, so that the body of Christ may be built up until we all reach unity in the faith and in the knowledge of the Son of God and become mature, attaining to the whole measure of the fullness of Christ" (Eph. 4:11–13).

OFFICE SPACE

Some of the executive roles volunteer lay leaders fill are on the church property, while others are in off-campus settings (such as in one's home). For executive lay staff who serve alongside paid professional staff, a similar work environment is a reasonable thing to expect. If a workstation or office is needed, the cost is minimal—compared to paying a staff member in a similar role. Another thing to consider is that an office gives visible credibility to the person and the work they are doing.

EXPENSE ACCOUNTS

While volunteers gladly donate their time, they should not be expected to pay for their volunteer service. For example, if a cell phone is needed, the church should provide it. If the pastoral staff gets reimbursed for business mileage, the same should apply for lay ministers serving in critical positions. The licensed lay minister officiating at a graveside service or a wedding should be treated the same way an ordained pastor would be treated.

RECOGNITION

Everyone appreciates a word of thanks, especially when much effort has been given. In Appendix B there are fifty ways to support and recognize volunteers.

CHAPTER 9

COMPETENT PASTORS

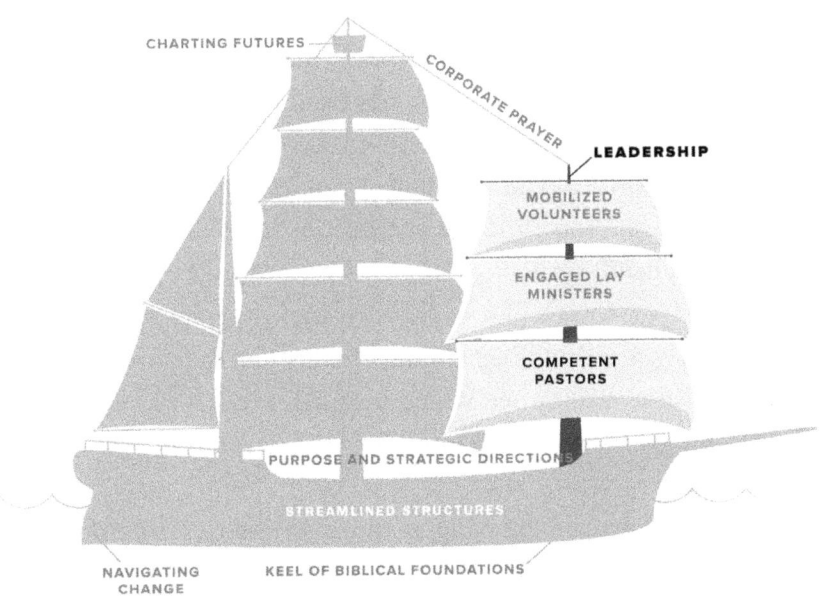

A healthy church embraces the biblical teaching that every member is a minister. And some of those who volunteer are able to go deeper in their engagement by actually serving as lay staff or lay pastors. Now we will look at the service role of those who minister in remunerated equipping, coaching, and pastoral capacities.

Competent Pastoring Is More about Leadership than Management

The third sail on the mast of leadership is Competent Pastors. If any position requires solid management skills, it is the pastorate. If a youth pastor, for example, plans a senior high snow retreat and only discovers at event time that transportation has not been arranged, the whole retreat is in jeopardy. The right kind of ministry execution requires a myriad of details, and someone has to manage it. More likely, several people are necessary to assure managerial excellence.

Nevertheless, competent pastors are more leaders than managers. Those at the helm of the ship have not been called primarily to oversee operations, but to set course directions. Leaders infuse vision; they set agendas and priorities. The last thing any of us want to hear when asking for directions is, "You can't get there from here." Leaders reject this. They are insightful, strategic, and perceptive. And they are persistent!

If leaders are too far out in front of their people, they are hard to follow. If they are huddling among the group, they are not leading. Leaders will not wait to see which way the wind is blowing. Though they are politically savvy, they move forward strategically based on their convictions.

When we consider the congregations we are familiar with, can we identify even one thriving, healthy, and growing church that is led by a mediocre pastor? I doubt we can. Pastoral excellence is essential for impactful ministry.

Competent Pastoring Is More about Communication than Preaching

Preaching is a significant part of a pastor's job, especially in solo pastorates and for lead pastors of multiple-staff teams. But preaching is just one type of communication. Most ministers, even teaching pastors, likely spend more time teaching, writing, talking, emailing, and texting (all forms of communication) than they do delivering a thirty-minute exposition.

Communication is holistic. In oral communication, we craft words, choose the appropriate tone, and use nonverbal expressions. The rate, pitch, and volume of speech can intentionally shift to captivate listeners. Words paint pictures, stimulating the intellect and touching the emotions. Competent pastors constantly strengthen their communication abilities, whether publically unpacking a biblical text or privately encouraging a new Christ-follower.

It is not uncommon in multigenerational congregations to see a difference of opinion regarding classical preaching. Older congregants who grew up with straight-line sermons that included a beginning, middle, and end can track with a sequential, didactic sermon presentation. But younger adults and youth growing up in a society of images and visual representations are less captivated by the classic sermon outline. Effective preaching reaching cross-generational hearers must use stories that captivate one's attention by creating mental images. Preachers need to communicate more like Jesus, who even today could capture the postmodern mind. And engaging speaking must push beyond the sermon into all of a pastor's methods for expressing ideas. Competent pastors are more concerned with effective communication than preaching.

Competent Pastoring Is More about Missionary Work than Chaplaincy Work

In one consultation, I asked a pastor, "What really rings your bell?" He quickly replied, "I marry, I bury, I do the sacraments. That's it." At the time he went to seminary, his school trained clergy as shepherds and congregational caregivers. This minister saw himself as responsible for his congregation. In essence, he was their institutional chaplain. He sensed no responsibility for the people across the street who did not attend his church.

If a missionary is asked, "What really rings your bell?" the response is likely to be, "My job is to reach every one of the people in this community with the gospel of Christ." This attitude is much more than mere congregational caregiving. I am not saying that pastoral ministry is not about shepherding. It is! But a church cannot experience maximum health if it fails to take the Great Commission seriously. Jesus told his disciples, "Go into all the world and preach the gospel to all creation" (Mark 16:15). Biblical leaders want to know what part of "go" don't we understand? Competent pastoring is more about missionary work than chaplaincy work.

Competent Pastoring Is More about Networks than Repositories

One hundred and fifty years ago, the most educated person in most towns was the pastor. Minsters were among the few people who owned private libraries. Of course, things have changed. Knowledge keeps expanding, and advanced degrees are now common in every field. For a period of time at the theological seminary where I taught, I was the only faculty member in the education and ministries departments. I taught courses in children's ministry, adult ministry, family systems, pastoral ministry, and leadership studies. All of these fields have developed significantly over the years. The seminary now offers a degree specializing in children's and family ministry, with nine specialized courses, including one focusing on children's advocacy. We now offer a degree in transformational leadership with specialized courses like team leadership and measurement-based leadership. Knowledge in most fields is exploding, as it is in leadership studies, and one person simply cannot serve as the repository of knowledge for everything.

The same explosion of knowledge affects congregational life. For example, an effective youth pastor is not the one who attempts to counsel parents on all issues. Instead, a good youth pastor is someone who knows when and how to refer parents and others to experts. He or she might say, "Here is an agency that can help you with that," or "Here are some great resources to help answer that question."

Effective pastoral ministry over the long haul requires a familiarity with available networks. A pastor need not start an AA group if a sister church across town has one. Nor does a pastor need to be an expert on blended families if there is a family in their church who has pulled that blending off successfully. Experts are all around us. In our congregations are financial planners, counselors, physicians, attorneys, focus-group facilitators, people developers, statisticians, teachers, leaders, architects, government workers, writers, and even book editors! And the list goes on and on. Pastors can never know enough, but effective ministers can connect people with the information they need. Strategic pastors are intentional networkers.

Effective Pastoring Is More about a Church's Future than a Church's Past

Entering the foyer of Hope Church, one first notices the photos of all their pastors since their founding nearly one hundred years ago. There are also posters of all the confirmation classes, with the confirmands declining in numbers annually. What this says very loudly is that "Our church history is very important to us; our past matters."

Adjacent to the foyer at Hope Church is a large library. One of their consultants recommended they relocate all of their historical material to the library. They agreed the historical things were important, but that is not who they are now or who they are becoming. The consultant then advised the church to take engaging shots of their nursery school, kids' clubs, student ministries, and even to take an aerial shot of the community. The idea behind the pictures, which would now be placed in the foyer, would proclaim: "This is who we are, and this is what we are about; the future matters to us."

Does the past matter? Of course it does. But for effective, competent pastors, a congregation's health is more about its future, than it is about its past.

In summary, the leadership mast has three sails. The degree to which they are unfurled impacts the effectiveness of a congregation. Healthy churches have mobilized volunteers who serve consistently. These are the frontline servants of the congregation—the saints equipped for service.[27]

Engaged lay ministers are volunteers who have accepted a deeper ministry role. Though they are not remunerated, they give significant amounts of time by accepting ownership for an area of ministry.

Finally, competent pastors are the called, gifted leaders who have the training and competencies to lead the congregation well. For them, ministry is not merely a job, but rather a divine calling. And like the apostle Paul, they will try every means possible to bring people to Christ.

Hoisting the Sails

MENTORS

All pastors can benefit from a mentor, a seasoned ministers perhaps a decade or so down the ministry road who has navigated successfully the pastoral journey. My advice to pastors is to find one or two of these veteran leaders, and listen. Also, a good compendium of sage counsel from forty-five of these colleagues can be found in my book, *Dear Pastor: Ministry Advice from Seasoned Pastors.*[28]

---

27   "So Christ himself gave the apostles, the prophets, the evangelists, the pastors and teachers, to equip his people for works of service, so that the body of Christ may be built up until we all reach unity in the faith and in the knowledge of the Son of God and become mature, attaining to the whole measure of the fullness of Christ" (Eph. 4:11–13).

28   John R. Cionca, ed., *Dear Pastor: Ministry Advice from Seasoned Pastors.* (Loveland, CO: Group Publishing, 2007). The complete book is available as a PDF file at *www. ministrytransitions.org.*

Peer Groups

A number of pastoral colleagues have praised the benefits of peer groups of pastors. A group of three to four like-minded colleagues can encourage, listen, advise, and even play together. Things that could not be shared with a church member, board member, or staff member, can be shared in confidence with a trusted colleague from another church. Peer groups can be assembled at pastors' fellowships, denominational meetings, or anywhere pastors gather. From that larger group, a few pastors who get along decide to meet weekly or monthly for fellowship. Often, senior pastors connect with other senior pastors, children's ministers with other children's ministers, and so on. Sharing with colleagues in a similar ministry role can provide valuable insights—and sanity.

Continuing Education

Books, classes, podcasts, conferences, and peer reviews can all build ministry competencies. Viewing sermons from different ministers can help a pastor learn from different preaching styles. This is important because it helps us find our own authentic voice. The pastor who quits learning will eventually quit leading.

Observation Days

Some churches allow the pastoral staff to take off one weekend each quarter to observe other ministries. This is not counted against their conference time or vacation time because these churches have found it valuable to stay abreast of how effective churches are serving their people and communities.

Annual Reviews

Congregants talk about how they think the church ministry is going, as well as how they believe the pastor is doing. This information is important for the pastor to know. Rather than endlessly speculating about what members are thinking, an official annual review by a supervising team can provide that information. But there are some specific dos and don'ts of pastoral assessment that should definitely be observed.[29] A review that is not handled properly can hurt more than help.

I'VE GOT YOUR BACK

As a young associate pastor, I made a BIG mistake one morning by making an announcement off a piece of paper that was handed to me just before the service began. I announced a basketball practice that afternoon at the church. Later that evening, an irate father subsequently cornered me, assailing heatedly, "Who the ____ do you think you are not letting my son play on your team?" I don't play basketball. I wasn't there. It wasn't my team. But apparently his son, a poor player, didn't have much on-court time that afternoon. Fortunately for me, my lead pastor saw what was happening, grabbed the dad around the shoulder, and pulled him into another room, saying "Chuck, we have to talk." He had my back. Over the years I have experienced other times of unmerited criticism, and I have been fortunate when elders have jumped in with "Pastor, we can handle this. Don't worry about it."

---

29   See Chapter Nine, "Pastoral Assessment," in *Before You Move: A Guide to Making Transitions in Ministry*, rev. ed. (Seattle: Create Space, 2011).

PART THREE

DYNAMIC COMMUNITY

CHAPTER 10

WINSOME FRIENDLINESS

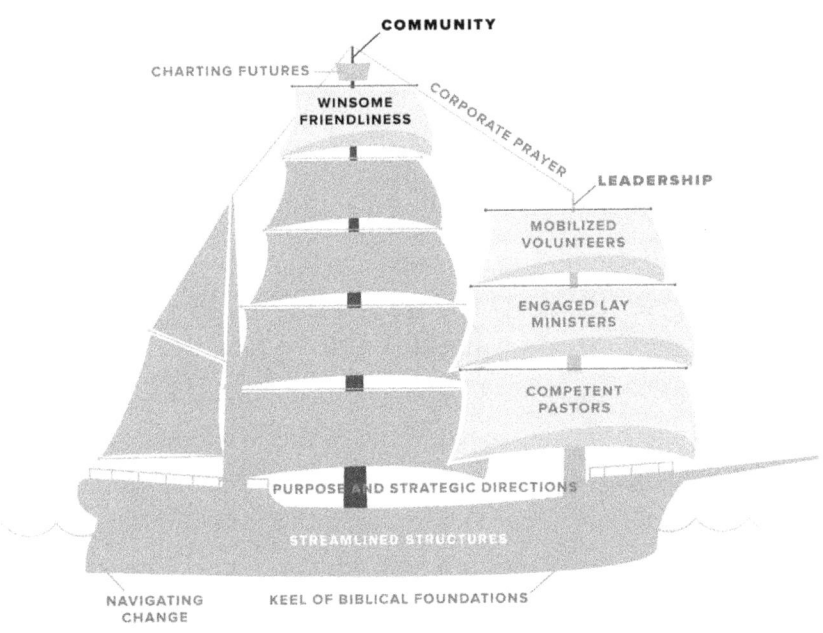

Dynamic Community is the center mast on the ship model of church health. Five sails, the five critical dimensions of community life, billow from that mast: Winsome friendliness, relational intimacy, awesome worship, transformational discipleship, and missional impact. These five factors represent the critical dimensions of the discipleship process.

Congregational maturity is best understood as a cyclical process. It begins with Christ followers acting like Christ in their communities. Their generally pleasing demeanor—winsome friendliness—draws outsiders to visit a neighborhood Christian group, Bible study, or church. They connect with people in a welcoming environment, and later they are nurtured and deepened in their faith. In turn, they sense a need to let others know what they have found in Christ, and in their church, so they are released back into the community to touch additional lives—and the discipleship cycle continues. This simple approach is the discipleship tactic the apostle Paul commended to Timothy: "And the things you have heard me say in the presence of many witnesses entrust to reliable people who will also be qualified to teach others." (2 Timothy 2:2).

Therefore, the first of the five sails, the topsail, is Winsome Friendliness.

Winsome Friendliness Is More about Thinking of Outsiders than Thinking about Insiders

We might be speaking Greek to outsiders visiting our church if we typically use terms like chancel, nave, and narthex. More subtly, if during the worship service we acknowledge Sara home from college, or pray for Brother Thompson who had a massive heart attack last night, or update people on the Clark's runaway niece, we may be guilty of insider trading. Of course, these warm announcements are intended for good, but they are still all about us. We are unintentionally thinking about inside family, not visitors. Without meaning to, we sometimes cultivate a we/they perception among our guests.

A church conducting a morning worship service as a family meeting will remain a small church. If a congregation's desire is to stay a small, intimate community, this approach will assure it happens. For a church wanting to grow, however, leaders know that drawing too much attention to insiders can feel exclusionary to outsiders. Keeping the service centered in God's goodness, mercy, and awesomeness touches insiders and outsiders alike. Announcements of a more personal nature can be made in a smaller group setting. These smaller venues provide more intimacy, are a great place for prayer support, and can facilitate discussions on how to assist those with particular needs.

Congregations that are winsome are congregations that are respectful of those who visit. They work hard not to embarrass outsiders. They go out of their way to welcome the outsider as when, for example, they reserve parking places for guests near the main entrance to the building. Labeling those parking spaces with "Visitor" signs is probably not a good idea because it emphasizes the "outsider" element and thus might make some visitors uncomfortable. A better practice is to simply educate the congregation with an occasional reminder like, "Remember, we don't park in the first row because those places are reserved for guests." One congregation striped their parking lot with yellow lines, except for the ten spots closest to their front entrance. Those stalls were striped white. The congregation knew that the white spots were for guests.

Asking visitors to stand during a service could for some people be tantamount to asking them to wear a flashing red light. Keep in mind that when guests are simply "checking out" a church, they appreciate a welcome and warmth, but many are turned off by too much attention. Outsiders are drawn to winsomeness, but they avoid what they perceive as intrusiveness.

God does not need praise from people. Even when we are silent, the entire creation shouts out to God in adoration. Even so, we need to praise him, for we are incomplete—not fully human—apart from praising the one who created us in his image. And this is true for believers and unbelievers alike, even if it is not recognized. The children of God will have millennia to sing God's praises, but for outsiders, the time to understand God's love, forgiveness, and blessings is now.

Winsome Friendliness Is More about Removing Barriers than Compromise

Many churches in the early "seeker-sensitive movement" were led by pastors who were deeply concerned with making their campuses places where the unchurched felt comfortable. The movement used culturally sensitive methods, along with current marketing principles, to reach those not active in or totally unfamiliar with church. To remove barriers and get seekers in the door, theater seats replaced pews. Sermons were shortened and used more illustrations, and they usually centered on self-improvement. Theatrics and musical entertainment were highlighted. State-of-the-art sound and lighting technology were used. Foyers expanded. Coffee shops and bookstores appeared. Kids' ministries flourished. And technology exploded. The movement away from stained glass windows, pulpits, and hymnals was intentional. "Give our church a try," was the invitation. "This isn't your grandfather's church," was the message. "We play our music loud, and we even stand during all the singing—just like at rock concerts." And post-World War II baby boomers came in droves.

Unfortunately, the new approach also had its drawbacks. Hymns about God were replaced with simplistic choruses about how much we need God, or how much we love the Lord. God's love and goodness were preached, but rarely did church audiences hear about God's holiness and justice. Expositional preaching was replaced with therapeutic preaching. The unchurched and the churched alike didn't need to carry Bibles anymore, since sermon texts appeared on large screens. Christian symbols were minimized, and crosses were either eliminated or relocated so as not to block the screen.

There were many egregious theological drawbacks to the seeker movement in its early manifestation. For one thing, some in the movement taught the unsound idea that Jesus will make one's life better and bring one material blessings—like a genie who will always give us what we want. Many seekers bought the goods the movement was selling, only to forsake Christ when he failed to deliver what they wanted.

As the movement matured, however, there was less theological compromise. A healthier balance developed in many seeker congregations. Instead of being seeker driven, the movement became more seeker sensitive. The cross and Christian art reemerged. Theologically rich music increased. And relevant, biblical communication deepened. Perhaps somewhere down the line key leaders figured out that unchurched people are not offended when they go to a restaurant and find food. In fact, that is why they go there. Nor are seekers surprised to find fuel at a gas station. Again, it is the likely reason they stopped there in the first place. So why should anyone think the unchurched would be surprised—or offended—to find a cross, praise songs, or a biblical message at church? Is that not why they pulled into the church's parking lot? Today, in most cases, it is about preserving Christian distinctives while at the same time eliminating hindrances that detract from the Christian message.

If we expect the congregation to stand at a particular time in the service, then we can invite them to do so or place an asterisk in the program noting when to stand. If we expect the Lord's Prayer to be spoken, the words should be provided in the bulletin or on a screen. We can use the term "foyer" instead of "narthex." And we can explain that the death of Christ makes us morally clean before God, rather than declaring we are "sanctified." Winsome friendliness is not about compromise; it is simply about removing barriers that hinder outsiders from moving closer to Christ.

Winsome Friendliness Is More about the Marketplace than the Campus

We have described winsome friendliness as it relates to the church campus and events that happen there. But in reality, winsome friendliness is far more about how Christ followers live in their communities than how they act at church.

Is it important for Christians to demonstrate warmth to guests on campus? Certainly! Is it important that childcare workers smile in the nursery, and return dry and content babies to their parents? Of course! Every positive thing a visitor experiences is like a piece of Velcro that binds them to the church. An inspiring celebration time, a good message, a smile from strangers, a clean-smelling bathroom, informative signage, and happy kids—all are like pieces of Velcro. And with each new positive experience, the connection to a new congregation gets stronger.

Having said that, winsome friendliness is still more about what happens in daily life than what happens on the church property. It is about the attitudes one displays, and one's demeanor at work and in the community. It is about becoming genuinely pleasant and appealing, not just exhibiting a Sunday-go-to-church kind of friendliness.

What this means in everyday life is that if we see a neighbor sodding his front yard, we go over and help. If a neighbor is going on vacation, we volunteer to collect the mail or cut the grass. If someone has an emergency, we assist, or if they need childcare, we jump in. If a boss needs someone to take point on a project, we cheerfully volunteer. If a coworker seems troubled, we listen. If a coworker's project fails, we encourage them. And if we are criticized or slighted, we are not offended. Winsome friendliness is about Christ followers being pleasing, appealing, and engaging in their daily lives. It is about a winsome smile and a cordial greeting.

In summary, a congregation's health is impacted—negatively or positively—by the winsomeness of its people. Whether at church, a health club, a community class, a sporting event, or anywhere else we might imagine being, we should consciously shine our lights to glorify our Father in heaven,[30] so that people might inquire about the hope that is within us.[31]

Hoisting the Sails

SMILE

Never forget the attractiveness of a smile. We have no qualms asking for assistance from a pleasant clerk, but are hesitant to approach someone with a scowl. A smile indicates that things are generally good and satisfactory; it is the first step of approachability, and therefore the gateway to relationships.

NEIGHBORHOOD ACTIVITIES

Pastor Randy Frazee suggests that Christians living in the same neighborhood or geographical region invite neighbors into their activities.[32] Whether playing kickball in a cul-de-sac, initiating a block party, or going to a sporting event, inviting outsiders to these types of events enables them to see the dynamic of Christian friendship. He even recommends that Christ followers keep a portion of their tithes and offerings for the missional work they do together in their neighborhoods.

MARGIN ASSESSMENT

The truth is, when we're pressed for time we rarely make connecting with others a priority. If we are behind on a deadline, we are slow to divert from a project. We avoid people, or maybe we get "short" with

---

30 "In the same way, let your light shine before others, that they may see your good deeds and glorify your Father in heaven" (Matt. 5:16).
31 "But in your hearts revere Christ as Lord. Always be prepared to give an answer to everyone who asks you to give the reason for the hope that you have. But do this with gentleness and respect" (1 Pet. 3:15).
32 Randy Frazee, *The Connecting Church, 2.0.* (Grand Rapids: Zondervan Publishers, 2013).

them, so we can return to our work. No one wants to spend time with someone constantly glancing at their watch. Busyness is a serious threat to winsomeness. Therefore, becoming an appealing person begins with enough self-discipline to make possible moments for others.

SHORT-TERM PROJECTS

Many people are more likely to volunteer to work on a physical project, such as building a Habitat for Humanity house, than visit a congregation on a Sunday. An easy way to meet and connect with them is by working on a community project. A relationship with outsiders is easier to cultivate when it is on neutral ground.

HOBBIES

Meeting new people is definitely easier when you and they share a common interest. Friendships can develop through such avenues as motorcycle clubs, radio-control flying clubs, book clubs, bowling leagues, quilting classes, and cooking schools. Being cordial and attentive to others while pursuing things of personal interest is a natural way for the winsome friendliness of Christ to flow into a community.

FITNESS ACTIVITIES

Like hobbies, fitness activities provide another vehicle for meeting new people. Friendships can develop at a gym, on a court, or in a pool. Christ followers can share a positive spirit and a smile with trainers, coaches, teammates, and even judges and referees.

CHAPTER 11

RELATIONAL INTIMACY

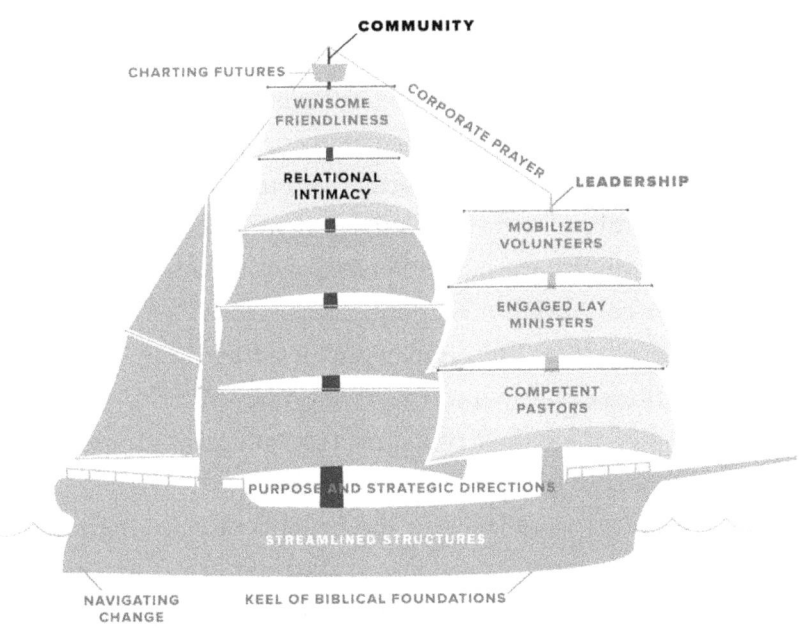

The winsome friendliness of our people and the role our church plays in the community can foster a welcoming culture. Many church campuses, for example, offer their facilities as places to vote. When couples start looking for a home church, many try the church they are familiar with from voting. Many churches are the centers for community blood drives. Some people start attending because the church was the site where they donated blood. Making our facilities available to the community is a great way to familiarize our campus to people.

Most often, however, newcomers first attend a church because someone they respect and enjoy invited them to visit. Winsome friendliness can draw people through a church's front door, but additional work is needed to keep them from leaving out the back door and never returning. Relational Intimacy is the factor that moves outsiders to the place where they feel like insiders. In the words of Leith Anderson, their new church starts feeling like "a place to belong, and a place to become."[33]

Before looking at the key principles of relational intimacy, it is important to recognize that people differ on the depth of relationship they want with others. For example, many newcomers prefer not to sign a friendship pad or a communication card during the worship service. They may go months without letting anyone know they have been attending. At this point, they prefer anonymity to intimacy.

Some are comfortable keeping most of their relationships at an acquaintanceship level. Others may pursue a friendship or two, perhaps because of some common interests. And some will risk a deeper friendship, where they share their concerns, risk vulnerability, are supportive of one another, and have each other's backs.

Most people can understand the benefits of close friendships, but their compressed schedules and fear of closeness keep them from investing in others. So how does a church strengthen connectivity—or in the words of Pastor Larry Osborne, how does a church increase its "sticky factor"?[34] There are three principles on relational intimacy to consider.

---

33   This was the branding slogan for Wooddale Church of Eden Prairie, Minnesota, during the years Leith Anderson served as their senior minister.
34   Larry Osborne, *Sticky Church* (Grand Rapids: Zondervan Publishers, 2008).

Relational Intimacy Is More about Smaller Communities than Larger Events

Events draw crowds. Whether the activity is a "weekend event," the term used by many churches for their worship services, or some other program, relational intimacy is hard to come by in larger venues. Larger venues require little self-disclosure, and they are great front doors to a church. Members can invite outsiders, knowing they will be welcomed and never embarrassed.

But getting to know people on a deeper, more private scale rarely happens in an auditorium, at a concert, or at some other large-group event. Connectivity requires smaller settings. Mid-size activities, where there might be an average attendance of twenty-five to forty, offer an easy way to become acquainted with a number of people. Smaller venues of eight to sixteen in size, enable participants to learn each other's "stories" and to come away knowing one another better.

Relational Intimacy Is More about the Home than the Church Campus

Somehow the home as a ministry site has been overlooked. The early church met almost exclusively in homes. For most congregations today, ministry happens at the church. After building multi-million dollar campuses, it is hard to justify a decentralized approach to ministry, where private homes and other off-campus sites are used for church purposes. Nevertheless, relational intimacy does not happen best on a church campus. Community happens around a table, in a living room, on a retreat, during a trip, or over a project. Informal settings are usually more welcoming, and therefore they invite connecting.

Men, for example, are less likely to open up to others in a formal situation.[35] One would be thought very strange walking up to an

---

35   David Murrow, *Why Men Hate Going to Church* (Nashville: Thomas Nelson, 2005).

unknown man and saying, "Come over here so we can sit down together and share." Yet, when two men spend four hours in a golf cart, they can talk about everything, even if their legs bump up against one another from time to time. This is what relational intimacy is all about. Men will hunt, fish, play sports, and build. We need to connect men to other men by inviting them to join us for the kinds of activities that bring them to life.

Relational Intimacy Is More about Connecting New People to New People than Connecting New People to Core Members

As described in the previous chapter, winsome friendliness is about noticing, relating to, and liking outsiders. Relational intimacy draws newcomers into the church's fellowship. Unfortunately, many churches have a revolving door, in that they find it hard to get recent attendees to stick. Even with intentional follow-up, newer folks seem to drift away after several months.

Some congregations, trying to strengthen connectivity, divide the names of newcomers among key church leaders for follow-up. But too often, even when using leaders with personal warmth and people skills, their efforts fail to retain guests. An analogy from Legos explains why that approach is flawed. Each Lego has a finite number of raised dots. When all the dots on a brick are interlocked to other bricks, that Lego is all snapped up. You simply cannot connect another brick to a Lego without any open dots, and you cannot force new connections.

People are like Legos in that regard. Some may have more relational capacity than others, but everyone has a finite number of dots. And once the dots are all interlocked, additional relationships are not very likely. We can be friendly and nice to other people (new dots), but realistically, we don't have the capacity to develop new relational connections. Thus, congregations successful in moving guests into the church community have discovered that relational intimacy happens better when connecting new people to new people. Newcomers to a church are not all snapped up, and they have room for new connections.

As I was leaving the auditorium at one church, I greeted a young couple I noticed. I learned it was their first Sunday at Grace Church. Just a few minutes earlier, nearer the front of the auditorium, I met a couple who said it was their second Sunday attending. I said to the first timers, "Don't go away!" I ran back and got the other couple, and took them over to the new couple, and said, "You all have to meet each other. This church has over four thousand people. The best way for you to connect is just to jump in with newer folks like yourselves. Why don't you go out to lunch together?"

Many people find relational intimacy and a place to belong in a class, on the course or courts, or in a special interest or affinity group. The principle is the same for the church: relational intimacy is more about connecting new people to new people rather than connecting new people to core members.

Hoisting the Sails

New-Attendee Luncheons

Many congregations follow the practice of inviting guests to a free luncheon. These once-a-month meals are a no-pressure way to informally meet those recently attending the fellowship. A word of greeting from one of the pastors is commonly given, but not much else. The purpose of the informal luncheon is hospitality, with some staff present to answer questions that may surface.

Meet-the-Staff Coffees

Some congregations provide an opportunity for guests to meet the church's pastor(s). This is usually an informal time between or after services. Other congregations mail a formal invitation to recent attendees, asking them to RSVP to an evening meal at the pastor's home or the home of one of the church leaders.

Here's Calvary Class

Calvary Church is an example of a church that shares the practice of many congregations offering a monthly Saturday morning class. The class gives an overview of the church's mission, values, program, and staff. Whether a newcomer ultimately is interested in membership or not, "Here's Calvary" is designed to provide the information they need to take a next step with the church.

Midsize Clusters

Many established congregations use adult Sunday school classes as part of their discipleship ministry. They see the classes as a good vehicle for both learning and fellowship. Younger churches, however, because of building costs and a more decentralized approach to ministry, prefer a small-group format for study and community. Interestingly, in the absence of these mid-size groups, a newer generation is now touting their value.[36] Whether mid-size communities meet weekly, monthly, or even quarterly, many leaders cannot fail to see the connectivity benefits of these groups. Worship services are too large for relational intimacy, and for many, small groups are too intimate for joining. Thus, mid-size activities, whether a regular class or a periodic activity, are surfacing again as an entry way for people to connect with others.

Affinity Groups

Affinity groups are gatherings of people who have common interests. People attend computer classes, quilting classes, and weight-loss classes.

---

36   Bob Hopkins and Mike Breen, *Clusters: Creative Mid-Sized Missional Communities* (Pawleys Island, SC: 3dm Publishing, 2007).

They exhibit their talents at art shows, display their cars at classic auto shows, and sell their produce at farmer's markets. A church can foster relationships within their congregation by connecting people with common interests. They can also use affinity groups to link outsiders with believers who have similar interests.

Life-Stage Activities

MOPS programs[37] have connected mothers of preschoolers for decades. Typically in a church setting, young mothers can make new friends and learn together, while their children are cared for during the two-hour bimonthly meetings. At many churches, single parents can find understanding, encouragement, and fellowship at seminars, classes, and socials. And seniors gather for hymn sings, special outings, and luncheons on a regular basis. A natural way for people to develop relationships is by meeting with others going through the same season of life.

Service Teams

Using one's strengths on behalf of others is more than an outlet for personal fulfillment. When people join together to serve, they draw closer together. Fellowship is more than anything a by-product of doing things in common.

---

37   http://www.mops.org.

CHAPTER 12

AWESOME WORSHIP

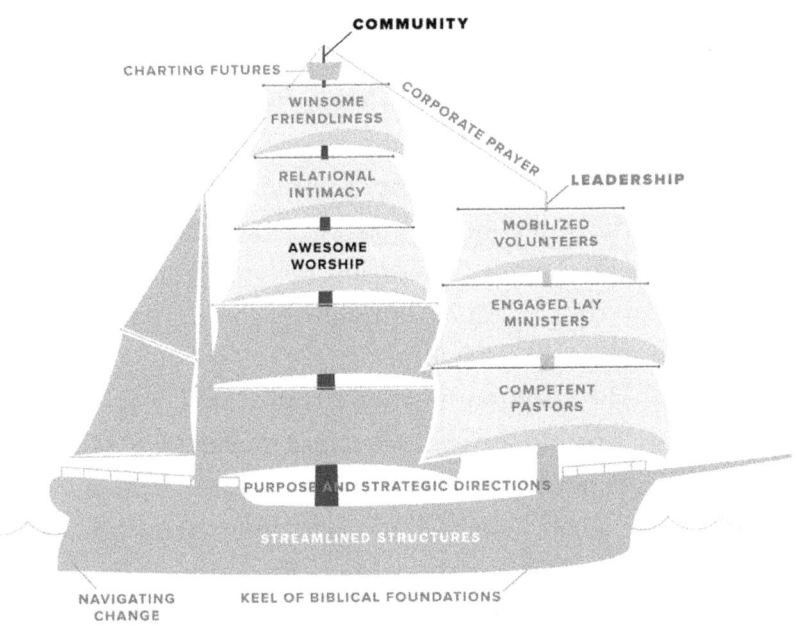

No area of church life has the potential for drawing people closer together, or alienating them further from one another, than church worship. Some churches maintain one established *form* of worship. In corporate terms, they are carving out a market niche by reaching out to specific groups within their community. Other congregations, in an attempt to reach a more diverse population, offer two styles of worship each Lord's Day. Typically, one service is traditional/blended, while the other is a praise/contemporary service. Some larger churches have differentiated their worship services even further. The range includes liturgical, traditional, blended, contemporary, and other styles. Some pastors even change their clothing between worship services, from a robe to casual dress or jeans, in order to fit the ambience of the service and the people attending.

Congregations also adapt their structures and facilities to accommodate the various preferences of their people. While many morning services are still in an auditorium with fixed seating, an increasing number of churches are moving to a sanctuary-*plus* format. One service will meet in the more traditional sanctuary, and a less formal service will meet in a family life center, multi-purpose room, or gymnasium. In addition, a number of churches run a live video feed to lounges, cafes, or food courts. And while pipe organs can still be heard in traditional churches, how congregations "do church" on a Sunday morning is becoming increasingly different.

With all the discussion about traditional worship services, contemporary worship services, attraction models, and so on, weekend worship formats nevertheless remain fairly similar. Most churches offer something like a half hour of music and announcements, and then a half hour sermon. When a special presentation is offered, the people involved (preacher, soloist, musicians, dancers, actors, worship team, Scripture readers) usually practice ahead of time to perform for the congregants. Except for participatory singing, the typical attendee is expected to remain quiet.

People entrenched in the so-called music wars argue over whether there should be hymns or modern worship choruses used in worship. They argue over whether church music should be soft or loud and whether stage lighting should be soothing or showy. They also argue over introducing too many new songs versus doing the same songs over and over. They argue about the familiarity of lyrics, musical instruments, choirs or bands, uplifted or folded hands, and even standing versus sitting. Have we lost perspective on what the big picture of worship is all about? Just as J.B. Phillips reminded us that "your God is too small," do we need to take into account that our understanding of worship is likewise too small?[38]

Healthy churches maintain a high view of God. They reserve the word *awesome* for God alone—not a pair of jeans, a football play, or a video. And they understand five dominant principles about worship: it is more about God than us, more a medley of theology than a collection of songs, more fully sensory than merely auditory, more about participation than performance, and more about a lifestyle than an event.

Worship Is More about God than about Me

The Creator of the universe made us a diverse people. In fact, complexity and diversity are stamped throughout the whole world. Since people have different preferences in everything, including food, clothing, housing, entertainment, and transportation, it should surprise no one that people have varied preferences for worship, and they have strong opinions about what they do and do not like.

This book does not discuss how cultural preferences are acquired, nor does it relate how neurological patterns habituate, making some worship styles emotionally and physiologically uncomfortable for certain individuals. Instead, this book looks at the bigger picture of what the Christian community looks like when God is praised and when diverse groups draw together with one voice in adoration of the King. It is noble when a congregation seeks a balanced blend of music pulled from the great orb of styles and enriched history. But if congregants are allowed to get feisty over what they do and don't like, or get upset that others

---

38   J.B. Phillips, *Your God Is Too Small* (New York: Touchstone Publishers, 2004).

enjoy another style, then this self-absorption misses the entire point of worship, which is that it is all about what pleases God, not us.

Several years ago a presenter at a conference derided country music. I found this rather interesting, particularly because his congregation was located in cattle country. During a break I asked him a question: "Does God enjoy country praise?" He thought for a moment, and then he admitted, "I think God enjoys all praise." He got that part right. While it is fine for a church primarily to do one style of music, it is not okay for people to believe God is praised in only one way. In his song "The Heart of Worship," Matt Redman says it well: "I'm coming back to the heart of worship, and it's all about you, Jesus, it's all about You."[39]

Worship is about adoring God, who is honored by all praise that comes from a grateful heart. We are free to orchestrate worship services accommodating generational preferences, or other preferences, but we must continually remind ourselves we are about worship, not entertainment. God is the audience; we are the instruments. Healthy churches remember that worship is more about God than about us.

Worship Is More a Medley of Theology than a Collection of Songs

Some people, including some pastors, view worship as the preliminary, minor event to prepare for the main event—the sermon. But this is a shortsighted view of worship and preaching, and it is definitely a misunderstanding of what we know about human learning.

If there is a main event during the Sunday morning service, it is the worship time itself, not the sermon. We can all recite the alphabet. Many remember the order of letters because of a tune we learned long ago and still hear in our minds. Words set to music are more easily retained than words just presented sequentially. Something in the chemistry of our

---

39 http://www.crosswalk.com/church/worship/song-story-matt-redmans-the-heart-of-worship-1253122.html.

brains facilitates the deepening of neurological patterns (memory) better through melody and image, rather than through straight verbiage alone.

Please note that I say this not as a worship minister, but as a teaching pastor who preaches each Lord's Day. The pastor who thinks his pearls exposited from the Greek will impact a life more powerfully than a biblical text in melody (especially one accompanied by image) is naive. And that pastor is plain foolish to think a weekly thirty-minute sermon will offset the value-formation of dozens of hours of CDs, radio, cable, and video programs imprinting the flock every week.

If we are truly concerned with taking a Bible message and using it to transform minds, then this is most powerfully accomplished when the entire morning service is thematically correlated. If the morning worship experience is just a selection of a couple of hymns, or the repetitious singing of a few favorite songs, then we miss the great dynamic of synergy. The best Christian music is theology with melody.

Therefore, in designing the worship experiences, those responsible for drawing the congregation together in praise have the same task as the morning preacher. Together they are communicating great life-changing truths to the people. We must continually raise the bar in our worship ministries to combine the soundness of theology with the most captivating medium. For many, the truths that stick deepest in their souls reverberate through their minds in song and image. Worship is more a medley of theology than a collection of songs.

Worship Is More Fully Sensory than Merely Auditory

God has given us eyes to see, ears to hear, mouths to taste, olfactory senses to smell, and bodies to feel and move. All of these senses draw us to God and can be used to praise his name. Most of us worship through the auditory gate; in fact, many people use the words *worship* and *music* interchangeably. Some churches, for example, have a minister of music, while others employ a worship pastor.

Certainly the auditory sense is powerful in capturing attention, stirring the heart, and imprinting the mind. But worship is holistic and goes way beyond music. We adore God when hearing of his goodness in song, and we can praise him personally through voice or instrument. But adoration is also stirred by and offered through other senses.

Let me illustrate. In my office hangs a picture of Jesus walking on water with the apostle Peter walking toward him. Peter is beginning to sink in the water. There are no words on the canvas, but the painting carries a powerful message. For decades, that painting has drawn scores of students and guests into moments of adoration of Christ.

Many churches are increasing the use of *imaging* in their services. Nature scenes are common. Some use video clips in the service, while others use photographs and sculpture to tell a story. We are told that in the American population, 20 percent are auditory learners, 40 percent are visual learners, and 40 percent are kinesthetic learners. Almost half our population learns best by touching, manipulating, moving, and experiencing. For all learners, especially these tactile learners, worship can also include movement. Worship is more fully sensory than merely auditory.

As a child, I remember using rhythm instruments in our Sunday school. I never preferred the triangle or bell, but I did enjoy the sandpaper blocks. Every kid got an instrument. Unfortunately, now that I am in big church, only a few people on the platform get to play with the blocks, drums, or instruments. Another kinesthetic expression of worship is clapping. Granted, not everyone is comfortable clapping, or raising their hands, for that matter. But for those who are comfortable with this form of expression, clapping offers an opportunity to put our physical self into worship. It can be used during a song or as an expression of appreciation after the song (a tactile "amen"). Movement, whether swaying or dancing to music, also allows people to express their praise.

Rarely are the senses of taste or smell used in our worship services. We can do better. For example, a pastor teaching on John 6, where Jesus feeds the five thousand, or Matthew 26, on the Last Supper, could arrange to have bread baking in the auditorium during the service. The smell would permeate the auditorium during the message, and the bread would be ready in time to commemorate the Lord's Supper. The warm, fresh loaves would infuse a multisensory impression of Christ's life on our behalf.

Worship Is More about Participation than Performance

For too many people, church is an event or an activity. They are there to view the proceedings, as though they were attending a play or concert. And while we may complain about this attitude, we are largely responsible for perpetuating the misunderstanding. The fixed seating in our auditoriums, for example, is arranged for everyone to see the performers. Morning services are comprised of a few songs, performed music (by a choir or praise team), announcements, a prayer or two, and a thirty-minute sermon. But where is the congregational participation?

Our reading of Scripture can become more dramatic when we become more inclusive. We can use responsive readings, antiphonal readings, or multiple readers acting parts from a text. When we use the "Prayers of the People" (O Lord, hear our prayer) offered by a congregant rather than the pastor, we expand the participation level of the whole church. When people share faith stories describing their spiritual journeys, worship services can become more inviting. And when we coordinate the work of visual artists, musicians, and dancers, we again involve more people from the faith community.

Because worship is more caught than taught, intergenerational worship is a great practice. We can begin by allowing the children to attend morning services, or at least a part of them. Kids can also read Scripture, collect the offering, or lead in song. Children and adults alike are captivated by services that are family friendly. Children, youth, and adults all benefit from worship that is more participation than performance.

Worship Is More about a Lifestyle than an Event

Unfortunately, worship is a once-a-week experience for most Christians. As we have just observed, it is less about participation than performance. It is a service somebody "puts on" for them. If asked when they worship, they would probably say "at 9:00 AM." But this is far too limiting a concept for real worship.

One of my pet peeves is when a worship leader says, "Let us now enter into worship." I want to respond by shouting, "Where has God gone? Haven't we been worshipping in spirit and truth throughout this week? Do you mean worship only happens in this auditorium?" Maybe I need to breathe in a bag.

Yet since worship is adoration of our great God, then esteeming him can happen in thought, word, and voice not only on Sunday morning, but also throughout the rest of the week. Worship is also multisensory. I can praise the Lord for a good meal when I smell the dinner cooking. I can thank him for joy when I see the laughter of a child. I can thank him for seasons when I rake leaves and smell their unique fragrance. And I can admire him for refreshing the earth when I smell a new rain shower.

The Greek word for worship is *latreia*. That word is used in Romans 12:1, where it affirms that presenting ourselves to Christ is our true and proper worship. The New International Version has it this way: "Therefore, I urge you, brothers and sisters, in view of God's mercy, to offer your bodies as a living sacrifice, holy and pleasing to God—this is your true and proper worship." Interestingly, other Bible versions translate the text as our "reasonable service" or "spiritual service." The King James Version, for example, has: "I beseech you therefore, brethren, by the mercies of God, that ye present your bodies a living sacrifice, holy, acceptable unto God, which is your reasonable service." In the New American Standard Bible we read: "Therefore I urge you, brethren, by the mercies of God, to present your bodies a living and holy sacrifice, acceptable to God, which is your spiritual service of worship." The Greek word *latreia* can mean either worship or service. In reality, if we have a full concept of worship, then we adore God for who he is whether praising him with our mouth or serving him with our hands—both are true forms of worship.

Spiritual formation happens in many different ways. For some, it happens when reading a devotional or attending a retreat. Some maintain the habit of daily Bible reading and prayer, while others journal their thoughts and memories. Some write songs or sing words of praise. For others, spiritual formation happens when helping someone on the highway change a flat tire. In reality, all of these things are beneficial for helping us treasure our God.

Praise can flow from any source. The businessman completing a noon basketball scrimmage can praise the Lord for a body that works the way God designed joints and ligaments to work. Adoration can also be expressed by the senior who is grateful for a piece of great key lime pie. If God made taste sensations possible by just putting a few taste buds on our tongues and the roof of our palates, we can be dazzled to think of all the complexity of his diverse creation. Praise can also flow from an exhausted mother who asks the Lord to take her bundle of energy and use him for building up the Kingdom. And adulation can also come from a schoolteacher reflecting on collecting her paycheck from the school system, but recognizing that she really works for God by showing her students a reflection of Christ.

Honoring God for who he is is not a thirty-minute activity on Sundays. Worship is more a lifestyle than an event.

Hoisting the Sails

Here are several specific ways to enhance worship awareness and practice it in a congregation:

THEMATIC CALENDAR

Use a six to twelve month thematic calendar to coordinate preaching and multisensory worship. Creativity, recruitment, and rehearsals require adequate lead time.

WORSHIP SONGS OR THE RADIO, DOWNLOADED, OR ON CD'S

Encourage Christ followers to listen to praise music throughout the week, thus facilitating the Word of God to richly dwell within them.

CELL GROUPS STUDYING A RESOURCE ON WORSHIP

In small groups and classes, use a book such as Chris Atkins's *The Isaiah Encounter: Living an Everyday Life of Worship*[40] to educate the congregation on the role of worship in our mission.

OFF-CAMPUS CELEBRATIONS

Celebration experiences should not be restricted to sanctuaries. They can happen virtually anywhere—outdoors, in storefronts, or in someone's backyard pool or living room. Smaller, decentralized venues for worship and teaching may become increasingly strategic in the future for reaching those who do not feel comfortable entering a church building.

DIFFERENTIATION

Where possible, we should use multiple styles of worship. Some people like predictability, so for them a liturgical service may be preferred. Others like spontaneity. In this case, there is no need to worry about a

---

40   Chris Atkins, *The Isaiah Encounter: Living an Everyday Life of Worship* (New York: Morgan James Publishing, 2016).

bulletin for them, and the format from week to week should be varied. Some people prefer anonymity, while others like engagement. And the list goes on. Movie theaters have shifted to multiplex operations, and restaurants have clustered into food courts. These industries and many others have discovered a cultural reality. We may want to apply these discoveries to how we design our church programs and where we can take them.

Visit Worship Services

Those who plan worship services, including the teams who lead them, are engaged in their own services week after week. Still, time should be made available for visiting and interviewing the leaders from churches known for dynamic worship. Such visitation is highly informative and motivational. It is worth consulting other leaders once a quarter, so a church's primary worship personnel can see what else is going on out there.

Demographic Studies

When considering the addition of another venue for worship, consider the preferences of people in your community through the use of demographic studies. Don't assume everyone wants an upbeat, rock style, and remember that younger generations tend to be more eclectic than most Boomers.

CHAPTER 13

TRANSFORMATIONAL DISCIPLESHIP

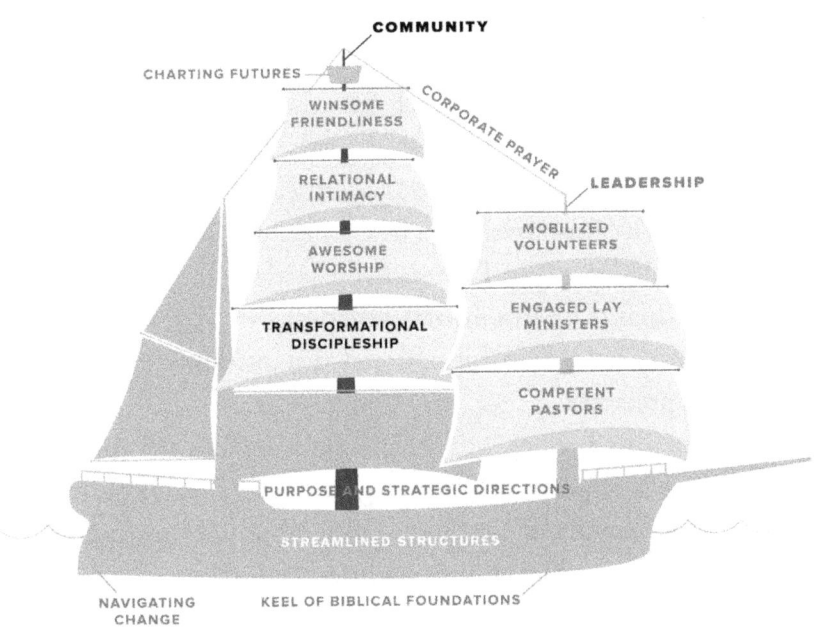

As we look at the mast of community, we ask first how winsome, friendly, and inviting are our believers. Then as people join us in community, they can develop intimacy and connect with others relationally. At first, some newcomers want space, but eventually they will sense a need to connect in order to grow. People develop in community, and a natural support network exists for those who are "doing life together." In the last chapter we considered the role worship plays in faith development. Now we will look at the fourth sail on this mast of community—Transformational Discipleship.

Transformational Discipleship Is More about Living One's Hardwiring than Practicing Disciplines

Transformational discipleship is more about living out one's hardwiring than practicing a set of spiritual disciplines. Transformational discipleship *is* about practicing the spiritual disciplines. Reading and meditating on Scripture is foundational. The Bible is God's revelatory disclosure of himself, and it is each Christian's GPS for life. The better we understand God and his Word, the better we understand ourselves. The Scriptures will impact our lives as long as we have breath. Prayer is also critical. We cannot walk the talk unless we are continually talking about our walk with the Father. Even fasting, journaling, and holy silence have their place in spiritual development. Nevertheless, personal spiritual formation—transformational discipleship—is not primarily about these practices.

Consider this further. Some Christians believe the mark of spiritual maturity is regular Bible reading. In fact, evangelicals distinguish themselves as "people of the Book." But what does spiritual maturity look like in the mainline church tradition? For many, it is social action and community impact. For the charismatic tradition, it is the Spirit's anointing. And in the contemplative tradition, it is people reflecting, journaling, or reading the desert fathers.[41]

---

41   For a study of these various traditions, see Richard Foster's *Streams of Living Water: Celebrating the Great Traditions of Christ* (San Francisco: Harper One, 1998).

Mature Christians look like and act the way God made them.[42] A spiritual Christ follower with the gift of teaching teaches. A believer with mercy gifts listens and cares. And a Christian wired with generosity gives liberally, encouraging others through his or her resources. The Scriptures teach that "we are God's handiwork, created in Christ Jesus to do good works, which God prepared in advance for us to do."[43] How did he prepare our works in advance? By the very DNA he placed in us, and by the experiences he brings into our lives.

In the final analysis, a fully devoted follower of Christ should look like the specific person God designed, appearing the way God made them, following after the heart of Christ, and using the spiritual gifts he has granted.

The classical spiritual disciplines can help us with personal and spiritual formation and becoming more like Christ. But transformational discipleship is not so much practicing the disciplines as living one's hardwiring. A disciplined approach to maturity alone is too restrictive. Spiritual growth is more the attitude, "Jesus, let me become what you designed me to be, and let me serve according to your design of my uniqueness."

Transformational Discipleship Happens More in Community than it Does Privately

Many sermons have impacted my life. The sermons that have had the most impact, however, were more inspirational than informational or transformational. Inspirational sermons cast visions, motivate, and sometimes they call for action. They can have information aspects, and sometimes they are even transformational, but usually the most effective type of one-way communication is inspirational.

---

42   A good explanation of this view of spiritual maturity can be studied in Arthur F. Miller, Jr.'s *The Power of Uniqueness* (Nashville: SIMA International, 2009).
43   Ephesians 2:10.

After being a professor for thirty years, I can say that the classroom setting is primarily informational. Occasionally a student would approach me after class and say, "Today's class was really inspirational; it was a such a blessing." That did not happen very often, because a lecture or discussion format is primarily informational. There can be some inspirational and perhaps some transformational pieces thrown in, but primarily the classroom is for informational purposes.

Transformational discipleship happens more in community than it does privately. For example, a group of women, or couples, who meet in accountability sessions can experience transformation over time. Sometimes group life is inspirational, and sometimes it is informational, but at its best, community life is transformational for its participants.

When looking at the mast of transformational discipleship, the fullness of that sail is determined by the number of people in a congregation who are actually doing life together. For some people, "church" is only a weekend event. There they may worship and learn, but rarely do they interact, discuss, ask questions, receive encouragement, or experience any of the important elements that define a church. If people are not serving in community, studying in community, or doing something in community, all personal and spiritual transformation is, at best, marginal.

Transformational Discipleship Is More about Availability than Conformity

Many churches assume what a mature Christian should look like. A mature Christian does this or that. A mature Christian is one who always prays with eyes shut or with hands open. But these things represent mere conformity and fall far short of describing actual spiritual maturity. At its center, spiritual maturity is an attitude that could be expressed like this: "Lord, help me become who you desire, and help me increasingly value what you value."

One shift I am seeing mostly among Boomers is a greater sense of the importance of Matthew 25, of keeping watch of the day and the hour. Many congregants in their fifties and sixties have contributed to church building programs, but now they wonder if more of their contributions should have gone into people rather than buildings. A number of pastors who built large churches are now sensing that they haven't really done as good a job as they could have of reaching their community—especially those trapped in a culture of poverty. It is now common in evangelical circles to see projects focused on helping people, like providing student backpacks, adopting elementary schools, tutoring, and working in all kinds of ways to show the presence of Jesus in their neighborhoods.

Transformational discipleship is never content with good weekend event attendance alone. "Wasn't it great that we had three hundred people here? We met the budget, so let's do it again next week." Yet that is not what transformation is about. Healthy churches may draw a crowd, but discipleship that is transformational is aimed at, and will only be satisfied with, people maturing in Christ.

In summary, transformational discipleship takes advantage of all the ways we can develop spiritually, including practicing the classic disciplines. But ultimately, transformational discipleship is simply about saying yes to the Holy Spirit as he guides our lives on a daily basis.

Hoisting the Sails

Gifts Assessments

Fully devoted followers of Christ will use the wiring, acquired skills, spiritual gifts, and life experiences God has knit into their lives. To do this in an effective manner, it is imperative that we become students of ourselves, paying careful attention to the work God has already done and currently is doing in our lives. For those in leadership positions, this means helping church members gain an understanding of their spiritual gifts and what part they play in building the Kingdom.

TRIADS

Some people have found one-on-one mentoring helpful in their spiritual development. Triads (groups of three) are perhaps even more beneficial, having additional advantages. Adding a third person in a group (and perhaps a fourth) adds additional experiences, produces greater collective insights, and increases encouragement and support.

SMALL GROUPS

Transformation happens best in community. The give-and-take, fellowship, support, and accountability of a small group contributes far more to spiritual development than passively hearing an exposition.

SERMON-BASED SMALL GROUPS

Sermon-based small groups key off the sermon delivered the previous weekend. Typically ten or twelve study questions are prepared each week to extend and apply the preached passage of Scripture. Many pastors have found a synergy in this two-pronged approach to study. A pastor will say, for example, "I will not discuss what happened to Paul in Thessalonica because you will have that in your growth group this week. I'll just tell you his instructions to the church this morning." People who only attend the Sunday service quickly realize they are missing out on the second half of the intended growth opportunity. And those who miss the sermon will view it online in order to prepare for their small group.

BIBLE-READING PLANS

For some Christians, a chart, devotional, computer app, or another type of resource helps with consistency in their private Bible study.

Having a specific reasonable-length reading each day makes their devotional time more achievable.

SHORT-TERM PROJECTS

Whether a short-term mission project or a service event in one's local community, when time and gifts are used to assist others, personal growth emerges. "What's that in your hand, Moses?" "What's that in your hand, David?" "What's that in your hand, Shamgar?" "What's that in your hand, Dorcas?" Whenever we use what God has entrusted to us, others are touched and we are transformed.

TEACHING A CLASS OR FACILITATING A GROUP STUDY

No matter what the topic of study, no one grows more than the teacher. A person wanting to know the Word of God better should teach the small group or class. Starting out as an assistant or apprentice teacher may be preferred by some, but just jumping in there, one step ahead of the hounds, is a great motivator for becoming a good teacher.

THE 1 PERCENT CHALLENGE

Jesus said, "For where your treasure is, there your heart will be also."[44] If our treasure is on earth, our hearts will be confined to the earthly. But if it is in heaven, then the heart will be concerned with the spiritual and the heavenly. Our hope, trust, and joys are there. If our treasures are laid up with God, then what we do with them for the Kingdom will be affected. Increasing one's generosity, even by only 1 percent for a year, contributes to personal spiritual growth. It makes the work of Christ a greater priority in our lives, and it increases our sensitivity to those with tangible needs. Several people I know have practiced the 1 percent challenge several years in a row until they reached a targeted stewardship goal.

---

44   Matthew 6:21.

CHAPTER 14

MISSIONAL IMPACT

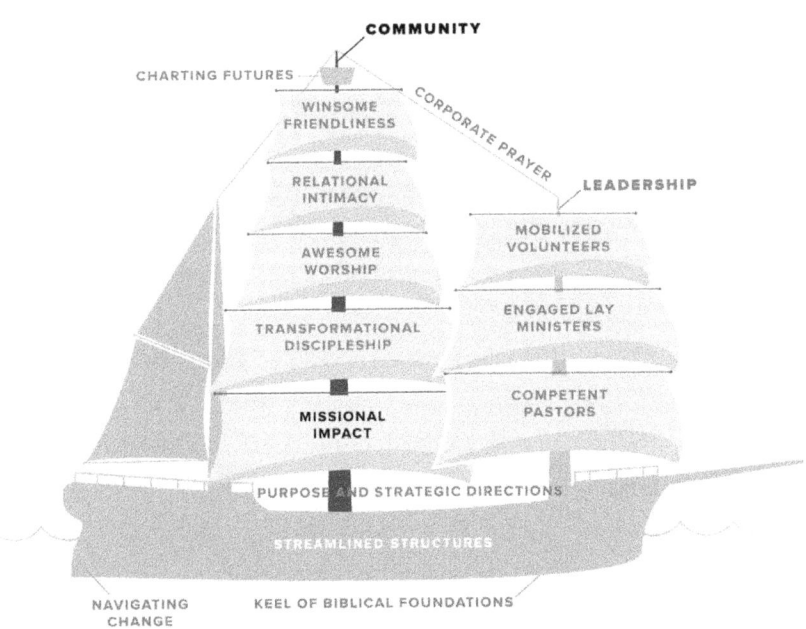

In this mast of community, we have seen people drawn into Christian fellowship, expressing together their praise to God, and growing deeper in their faith. But becoming fully devoted followers of Christ does not stop there. Authentic faith is more than personal spiritual formation; it is about being sent by Christ into the world to set up his kingdom. This involves our neighbors. The Lord told us in the Great

Commission to "go and make disciples of all nations, baptizing them in the name of the Father and of the Son and of the Holy Spirit, and teaching them to obey everything I have commanded you. And surely I am with you always, to the very end of the age."[45] The end of the world is coming, and all earthly kingdoms will be delivered up to God. Until then, we are to be about loving and reaching those apart from Christ.[46]

Christianity has no end-users. In the words of the Apostle to young Timothy, "The things you have heard me say in the presence of many witnesses entrust to reliable people who will also be qualified to teach others."[47] We have to train reliable and faithful men and women to continue advancing God's kingdom. The gospel was committed to us as a sacred trust, not to hold on to, but to pass on to others. Four generations are identified in this text: the apostle Paul, the disciple Timothy, reliable people, and other reliable people. No one was ever meant to be a consumer, or end user, of the gospel. That was never Christ's design for his bride.

Every blessing a believer receives is designed to be shared with another. This is the meaning of being a "steward," one who serves and cares for the welfare of others. In 1 Peter 4:10, we learn that "Each of you should use whatever gift you have received to serve others, as faithful stewards of God's grace in its various forms." All natural abilities, all acquired skills, and all spiritual enablements exist for others. Therefore, the last sail on the mast of community is Missional Impact.

45　Matthew 28:19–20.

46　"'Love the Lord your God with all your heart and with all your soul and with all your mind.' This is the first and greatest commandment. And the second is like it: 'Love your neighbor as yourself.' All the Law and the Prophets hang on these two commandments" (Matt. 22:37–40).

47　2 Timothy 2:2.

Missional Impact Is More about the Person than the Soul

It is not that missional impact is not about the soul. "Soul winning," to use an old expression, is at the heart of the gospel. In fact, lost people matter to God so much that he gave us three parables to emphasize the point.[48] Scripture is clear that even those apart from God are a priority to him. Therefore, Christ followers are concerned that people who have not received the gospel message of salvation be presented with it to have the chance to decide to follow Jesus as their Savior and Lord. This is eternally huge! The principle that missional impact is more about the person than the soul does not dilute the importance of a person repenting of sin and turning in faith to Christ. Without this commitment, there is no eternal life. But most people need to see the reality of Christ before they are willing to make a commitment to Christ. And Jesus Christ is embodied in people.

Evangelism—outreach—must be holistic in nature. Authentic Christlikeness means being concerned with the people, and not just what spiritual decision they make. It is not about building a relationship as a cover so we can present the gospel to them. It is about building a relationship with them, being committed to them, because they matter. They are people created in the image of God, and he dearly wants them to know about his love. It is about being there for those whom Jesus loves, for the rest of their lives, as long as they are neighbors—whether they trust Christ or not. It is about using the blessings God granted us in order to bless others. It is more about the whole person than the soul.

Missional Impact Is More about Neighborhoods than the Church Campus

As I said previously, relational intimacy is more likely to happen off the church campus than on. In the same way, the missional impact of

---

48   The parable of the lost sheep, the parable of the lost coin, and the parable of the lost son. All appear in the gospel of Luke, chapter fifteen.

reaching the unchurched is more likely to happen in our neighborhoods than on the church property.

Some readers may disagree. They might cite, for example, a megachurch with an eleven million dollar youth complex and a four million dollar fitness center. I know the church. I have been there. And I agree that they do a marvelous job when it comes to missional impact. Much of that church's effort is given to drawing the community in to use their space. But this ministry is an anomaly among the 340,000 congregations in America.[49] The church campus is very important. We can invite Weight Watchers, Boy Scouts, and Alcoholics Anonymous to use our facilities—and we should! Yet we are more likely to minister to our neighbors in their neighborhoods than on our campuses.

Missional impact requires that we always consider outsiders when planning activities. Perhaps church leaders sense a need for a finance class for young couples. Pause for a moment. Do you think there are any unchurched young couples who could also benefit from a class on finances? Of course! Might a congregation have a need for a seminar on parenting teenagers? Again, could any unchurched people desire some pointers on the same issue? Sure! But typically, we offer our classes, discussion groups, and seminars only for our church insiders. Is there any reason to fear having outsiders join us in our churches? I don't think so.

Another possibility is to locate classes and seminars in a neutral zone rather than on our church campus—perhaps at a YMCA or in an office building. Our people could drive to this public place, and so could their neighbors. Outsiders are more likely to join a neighbor at a public place than at their church. And Christians are also more likely to invite a neighbor to a neutral environment than to the church campus. Some want to avoid the impression of pushing their faith on others.

Many unchurched people have a deep sense of compassion wired in them. They also have natural talents and acquired skills that they are

---

49   http://hirr.hartsem.edu/research/fastfacts/fast_facts.html#numcong.

comfortable using. A church's missional strategy should recognize this reality. An unchurched neighbor might more easily join the men in a congregation to build a Habitat home or to help paint a widow's house, than accept an invitation to attend a worship session. Rather than rigidly embracing the insider/outsider mentality, we need to move into our communities to work together with our unchurched friends to touch the lives of people. A by-product of working together is that they might also see the reality of Christ working alongside of them.

Finally, a comment on the future is also pertinent to this principle. In a country with growing expenses and deepening debt, church property one day may no longer be considered off-limits to taxation. When churches are required to pay property tax, congregations with the largest footprint will be hit the hardest. The argument will go something like this: "If your church doesn't pay property tax, and our township is providing police, fire, and other services (for which other businesses pay taxes), then the church is in essence receiving a subsidy. However, separation of church and state doesn't allow the public support for religious organizations. Therefore, your church will have to pay property tax just like any other business would."

Of course church campuses are important. A place to gather is great! But the Great Commission tells us we are to make disciples in our going.[50] Missional impact is more about our neighborhoods than our campuses.

---

50 "Therefore go and make disciples of all nations, baptizing them in the name of the Father and of the Son and of the Holy Spirit" (Matt. 28:19).

Missional Impact Is More about Team Outreach than Individual Service

There is something commanding about a team of people unselfishly helping others. A teamship endeavor has a greater effect than individual acts of kindness. If I assist someone, they may just think I am a nice guy. But if four or five Christ followers team up to help a neighbor, or start a neighborhood soccer game, they can also see the relationship we have with one another. The joy and friendship among the team of friends is a more powerful witness than even the completed project on behalf of the recipient. In fact, Jesus said the proof of his transformative power is the love his followers have for one another: "A new command I give you: Love one another. As I have loved you, so you must love one another. By this everyone will know that you are my disciples, if you love one another."[51]

Rather than personally serving at a homeless shelter, or a food shelf, or raking leaves for a neighbor, invite a small group of other Christians to engage in that service along with you. Missional impact is more about team outreach than individual service.

Missional Impact Is More about Entrepreneurial Expression than Set Strategies

When we considered the sail of mobilized volunteers, we saw the importance of serving out of one's gift mix. Can a church engage in forty days of this or fifty days of that? Sure. All-church events can serve an important purpose. But inviting everyone to journal, share the gospel with a particular tool, or join in on one project does not capitalize on individual passions, strengths, and experiences.

God made some people great with numbers, so let those people team up to assist neighbors with income tax preparation. Other people

---

51   John 13:34-35.

were created with the ability to work well with their hands; these people could help build homes, or rebuild a damaged home. Some have an excitement about technology, which would lend them to helping seniors with computer needs. These suggestions for matching gifts with ministries are natural, not forced. Outreach is natural when we use the wiring God put into us already.

Missional Impact Is More about Eternity than Temporal Well-Being

Missional impact is about giving a cup of cold water *in Christ's name*, not just giving cold water. As Matthew 10:42 states, "If anyone gives even a cup of cold water to one of these little ones who is my disciple, truly I tell you, that person will certainly not lose their reward." As Mark 8:36 asks, "What good is it for someone to gain the whole world, yet forfeit their soul?"

Missional impact is about balance. Balance is the counterpoint between the whole person and the soul.

In summary, missional impact is not asking people to do something they have no inclination for and no passion for. It is not asking them to do something that is distant to their interests and abilities. Rather, it is asking people simply to take what God already wired into them and release that, not just for the body of Christ, but for the community as a whole. That's missional impact at its best!

Hoisting the Sails

Sharing Tools

Most neighbors do not have all the necessary tools or equipment to maintain a home. Young families especially are limited when it comes to things like hedge trimmers, ladders, wheelbarrows, extension cords, weed whackers, and so on. By middle adulthood they may have acquired some of these, but almost everyone will still run into something they need to borrow (such as a valve stem puller for a shower or a basin wrench for a faucet). Whether sharing a drain router or a rototiller, a Christ follower who is generous with his or her tools makes a good neighbor.

SHARING ABILITIES

Even if a neighbor has tools for nearly every project, he or she may lack the know-how, or the confidence, to tackle it. Dropping a tree or replacing a toilet is far less expensive if one doesn't have to hire a professional for the service. Having a chain saw is one thing. Offering to tie off the tree and drop it for a neighbor is one step better. Besides, when you assist, you can be sure it doesn't fall on your home.

LOVING THEIR KIDS

Many young families do not have grandparents who live nearby, and some do not even live in the same time zone as their grandparents. In most communities, 82 percent of our neighbors are dual-income families, and have little margin. When they move from the newly married phase of adulthood to becoming parents of young children, they are frequently overwhelmed by their added responsibility and their diminished time and energy. Christians can offer their neighbors some extra free time by watching their kids. They can let the little ones play with their dog. They can let them join their kids or grandkids in activities. Jesus said, "Let the little children come to me."[52] Christ followers can be the arms of Jesus to neighborhood children.

PICKING UP EXTRAS

One Christ follower I know likes to frequent a bakery. Occasionally when purchasing bread, he will pick up a small loaf or two of specialty

---

52 "Jesus said, 'Let the little children come to me, and do not hinder them, for the kingdom of heaven belongs to such as these'" (Matt. 19:14).

breads for a shut-in neighbor. Another friend occasionally buys extra boxes of diapers when purchasing supplies for his grandkids. At his life stage, with the mortgage paid off, he can afford it. But for the young families receiving the gifts, it is a big deal.

QUALITY HAND-ME-DOWNS

Young children will outgrow their clothes before they outwear them. Rather than selling quality items in a garage sale, or giving them to a thrift store, why not make them available for free to neighbors? Despite the need level of recipients, quality clothing is always appreciated.

INVITATIONS TO CHURCH

Most people will say they visited a church because a friend invited them. Some churches target non-attenders four to six times a year, when the services are especially seeker friendly. During these times, business-size cards are available to members for handing to friends. Some churches use a special Web link with creative invitations that congregants just have to forward to their unchurched friends. Some churches time their outreach Sundays with the start of a new series on the family, or finances, or relationships. Many make Christmas Eve a particularly welcoming time for guests.

INVITATIONS TO COMPASSION SERVICE

The first Saturday morning of each month, the students at Conerstone Church collect canned goods for a local food shelf. On the preceding Wednesday evening they will have gone door-to-door in a two-block radius around the church inviting neighbors to set out goods on Saturday if they want to contribute. Over the years, the students have collected a lot of food for the needy. But equally important, the good demeanor of these teens has also resulted in occasional calls to the church office commending the church's compassion. One caller told the pastor that the young people asked if there was anything she wanted them to pray for. After she shared a concern, they prayed for her right there. Young people can be great ambassadors for Christ.

Neighborhood Studies

Tom and Barbara reached out to five young couples to see if they were interested in starting a neighborhood Bible study group. None of the invited couples attended church, though almost all had religious backgrounds. Now that they were having children of their own, their interest in spiritual things was rekindled. Over a period of three years, Tom and Barbara led each of the couples to Christ. When a new pastor arrived at their church, Tom invited these families to visit. All joined within four months and became active in the life of the fellowship. Within a few years, several of these new believers assumed leadership roles at the church. Two became deacons, one a preschool director, and one couple became missionaries to Guam.

Assisting with a Project

Some projects seem so large that the work appears overwhelming. Yet one's spirit is encouraged when a friend comes alongside to give a hand. Offering to assist with gardening, painting, tutoring, cleaning, driving, or even recruiting volunteers spreads the work across a couple more shoulders and is a welcomed Christian gesture.

Affinity Groups

I have said that affinity groups are a great way to connect people within the congregation who share a common interest. Affinity groups are also a great way to attract outsiders to insiders. A Christ follower can naturally invite a neighbor to show off his classic car in the church parking lot or exhibit her painting at the public library at an art show sponsored by the church.

PART FOUR

ESSENTIAL RESOURCES

CHAPTER 15

GENEROUS STEWARDSHIP

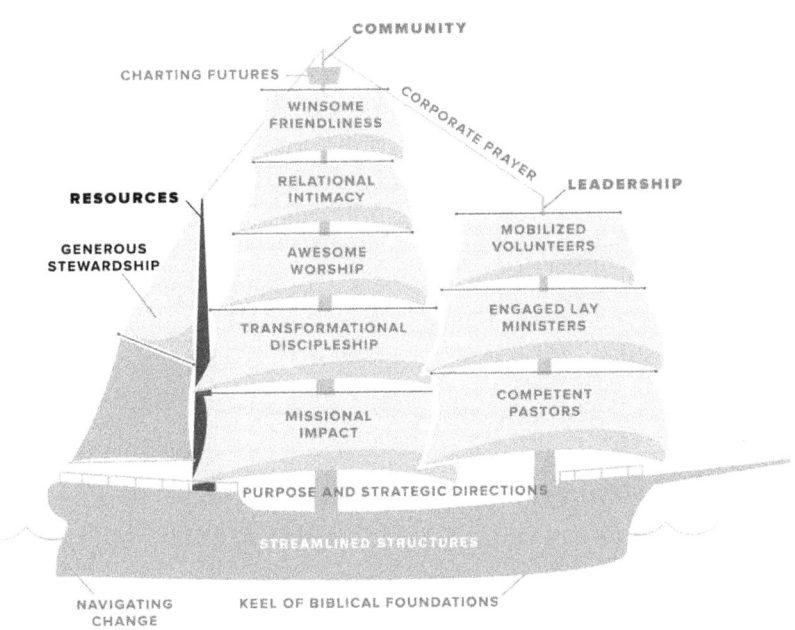

Frequently I conduct focus groups to discover the concerns of people in various communities. Regardless of geography or stage of life, two concerns repeatedly rank highest. Relationships and financial matters tend to consume the time, effort, and emotional energy of the majority of the people I have surveyed. People are worried about underemployment, debt, job security, tuition expenses, rising medical costs, and limited retirement income.

Expenses can easily rise to outpace income if we are not careful. Church leaders, therefore, should seriously ask why anyone would voluntarily give money away. Generous stewardship does not happen by accident; Christians become responsible givers when they understand several principles.

Generous Stewardship Is More about People's Need to Be Generous than a Church's Need for Money

Obviously, churches need financial resources. After all, money fuels ministry. Contributions convert into pastoral care and focused ministries. But the bigger issue here is that God wired us to give. Just as a healthy tree bears fruit, so, too, spiritually healthy people are generous toward others. Their fruitfulness flows through their gifts and abilities, but it also expresses itself through the sharing of financial resources.

Jesus taught a principle of reversed blessing: "For whoever wants to save their life will lose it, but whoever loses their life for me and for the gospel will save it."[53] And he practiced that principle every day: "For even the Son of Man did not come to be served, but to serve, and to give his life as a ransom for many."[54] Contrary to cultural media hype, we are not ultimately fulfilled by promoting and pampering ourselves. That sort of "satisfaction"—satisfaction by acquisition—has a short shelf life. More "stuff" does not produce deeper joy or greater significance. It is in giving that we receive.

God wired people relationally and designed us for fellowship. In the beginning of Scripture, we learn that, "It is not good for the man to be alone."[55] In community, we find identity and meaning. It is through contributing our talents, time, and treasure that we find significance.

---

53   Mark 8:35.
54   Mark 10:45.
55   "The Lord God said, 'It is not good for the man to be alone. I will make a helper suitable for him'" (Gen. 2:18).

In the words of Proverbs: "The generous will themselves be blessed."[56] Spiritual growth and personal joy are gained by investing in others.

Generous Stewardship Is More about Eternal Investing than Temporal Portfolios

In our first two decades of life, we spend most of our time in school. During the twenties and thirties, most people begin building a career, and, for many, a family. Since the period during our sixties and seventies is usually for retirement, most people work hard saving for retirement during their forties and fifties. Yet building a portfolio to live comfortably for one's remaining years is too shortsighted. The Bible teaches we are immortal, and though our physical shell will one day fall away, our inner person—our real self—will live on forever.

An old expression states that "You can't take it with you." That is both true and false. Of course, none of our earthly accumulation can be physically taken beyond the grave. But investments made in the Lord's work will last forever. Jesus put it this way: "Do not store up for yourselves treasures on earth, where moths and vermin destroy, and where thieves break in and steal. But store up for yourselves treasures in heaven, where moths and vermin do not destroy, and where thieves do not break in and steal."[57] Christians who truly understand long-term investing realize the importance of generous investing on the eternal level.

Proverbs teaches, "A good person leaves an inheritance for their children's children, but a sinner's wealth is stored up for the righteous."[58] A valid question, however, is how much money do our children need? And could too much unearned wealth spoil them?

---

56   "The generous will themselves be blessed, for they share their food with the poor" (Prov. 22:9).
57   Matthew 6:19–20.
58   Proverbs 13:22.

Many parents are now establishing a settled amount of money they will be leaving their children. They designate from their estate an amount each child will inherit, and the remainder of their assets is designated for ministries building the kingdom of God.

With so many people around the globe in spiritual darkness, many of whom are poor and disenfranchised, committed Christians are not at peace squandering all of their resources on themselves. And while they are interested in giving their children a head start through a significant gift or investment, they want them to understand that things of value come by hard work. Therefore, intelligent and generous stewardship is about eternal investing, not temporal investing. For many Christians, it makes sense to develop a kingdom investment portfolio into which they make deposits throughout their lives.

Generous Stewardship Is More about Proportional Giving than Tithing

Christians who know the grace of God in their hearts want to be gracious in return. They understand the principle, "Freely you have received; freely give."[59] The issue for them is not *should* we give, for that is a given. But many struggle with *how much* we should give, for the answer to that question is not explicit in Scripture.

Some churches teach the standard of *tithing;* that is, 10 percent of one's income should be given to the church, a religious organization, or to charity. But that principle is often misunderstood and may be too limiting. Old Testament believers practiced both *required giving* (tithing)[60] and *freewill giving.*[61] Furthermore, three specific tithes are

---

59   "Heal the sick, raise the dead, cleanse those who have leprosy, drive out demons. Freely you have received; freely give" (Matt. 10:8).
60   "A tithe of everything from the land, whether grain from the soil or fruit from the trees, belongs to the Lord; it is holy to the Lord" (Lev. 27:30).
61   "And the people continued to bring freewill offerings morning after morning. So all the skilled workers who were doing all the work on the sanctuary left what they

identified within the required giving: *the Levitical tithe,*[62] *the festival tithe,*[63] *and the poor tithe.*[64] To practice in a literal way, the Old Testament principle of tithing would require a tithe of 22.5 percent of one's income, not counting the freewill offerings to be made.

Unfortunately, a tithing mentality allows some Christians to think that since 10 percent belongs to God, they are then free to spend the rest on themselves. But we are stewards, not owners. "The earth is the Lord's, and everything in it, the world, and all who live in it."[65] In addition, Deuteronomy tells us that God is the one who gives us the ability to produce wealth.[66]

A more universal stewardship plan (beyond Israel's theocracy model) is found in the New Testament. To a number of churches, Paul gave this basic principle: "About the collection for the Lord's people: Do what I told the Galatian churches to do. On the first day of every week, each one of you should set aside a sum of money in keeping with your

---

were doing and said to Moses, 'The people are bringing more than enough for doing the work the Lord commanded to be done'" (Exod. 36:3–5).

62   "I give to the Levites all the tithes in Israel as their inheritance in return for the work they do while serving at the tent of meeting" (Num. 18:21).

63   "You must not eat in your own towns the tithe of your grain and new wine and olive oil, or the firstborn of your herds and flocks, or whatever you have vowed to give, or your freewill offerings or special gifts. Instead, you are to eat them in the presence of the Lord your God at the place the Lord your God will choose—you, your sons and daughters, your male and female servants, and the Levites from your towns—and you are to rejoice before the Lord your God in everything you put your hand to" (Deut. 12:17–18).

64   "At the end of every three years, bring all the tithes of that year's produce and store it in your towns, so that the Levites (who have no allotment or inheritance of their own) and the foreigners, the fatherless and the widows who live in your towns may come and eat and be satisfied, and so that the Lord your God may bless you in all the work of your hands" (Deut. 14:28–29).

65   Psalm 24:1.

66   "But remember the Lord your God, for it is he who gives you the ability to produce wealth, and so confirms his covenant, which he swore to your ancestors, as it is today" (Deut. 8:18).

income, saving it up, so that when I come no collections will have to be made."[67] In a follow-up letter, he wrote that gifts should be according to what one has[68] and what one has decided in his or her own heart.[69]

As we prosper, we should be able to give a greater percentage of our money away. Ten percent is a lot of money for a person with a $15,000 salary, but even 15 percent of a $200,000 salary leaves a lot of after-tithe discretionary income.

Realizing that "this world is not my home, I'm just a-passing through,"[70] we do not need to escalate our lifestyles. Increases in wealth can be assigned to one's kingdom investment portfolio. This is why the New Testament principle of setting aside money each week as the Lord prospers us is a better guideline for those living in an age of affluence.

Generous Stewardship Is More about Ministry Opportunities than Operational Needs

Many church budgets are pretty much black holes. No matter how much money is thrown into it, there is always more need. Besides some members not knowing what their pastors do all week, or what specific programs are provided by the church, they do not know and sometimes do not care how much money is spent on things from missions to maintenance.

Why do many churches have financial shortfalls? Perhaps the budget was set unrealistically high. Perhaps members withhold financial gifts because they disagree with specific programs. Maybe members have decided they do not want to fund what they think of as incompetence

---

67   1 Corinthians 16:1–2.
68   "For if the willingness is there, the gift is acceptable according to what one has, not according to what one does not have" (2 Cor. 8:12).
69   "But since you excel in everything—in faith, in speech, in knowledge, in complete earnestness and in the love we have kindled in you—see that you also excel in this grace of giving" (2 Cor. 8:7).
70   Albert E. Brumley, Acclaim Music, 1952.

or ineffectiveness. A shortfall may be present simply because of mismanagement. Giving to an operational need is not particularly the most motivating thing one can do.

On the other hand, when people see how ministries make specific kingdom impact, they are more willing to support effective work. For this reason, many advise reminding the congregation every time an offering is taken of a particular ministry the church supports. One might take this approach: "Wasn't that a great time of worship? As we receive this morning's offering, let's remember that your faithful giving makes possible the music ministry of our congregation." Or: "You may have noticed this morning that the front left side of our auditorium is relatively sparse. Seventy of our young people are away at a retreat this weekend, and we want to remember them in prayer. As the ushers come forward to receive our offering today, I want to encourage you to continue giving generously to our church. A part of your regular giving supports our outreach ministry to our youth, our future leaders."

The point is that people are more willing to give when they know where their money is going. No one is really excited about giving generally to *the church*. But people will give to targeted ministries, and to a general church budget, when they can see with some specification how they are helping the Lord's work advance.

Generous Stewardship Is More about Long-Term Viability than Annual Budgets

Whether we are thinking about the sort of stewardship the ant displays when storing its provisions,[71] or God's counsel to Joseph to reserve grain for the coming seven years of Egyptian famine,[72] steward-

---

71 "Go to the ant, you sluggard; consider its ways and be wise! It has no commander, no overseer or ruler, yet it stores its provisions in summer and gathers its food at harvest" (Prov. 6:6–8).

72 "It is just as I said to Pharaoh: God has shown Pharaoh what he is about to do. Seven years of great abundance are coming throughout the land of Egypt, but seven

ship over the long haul is commended. Some church leaders, however, think that saving for a rainy day is a secular notion and of no concern to the church. In fact, I have heard some Christians say their church spends every penny in the budget each year. The reason for this is that if they carry over a surplus into the next year, they might not trust the Lord to provide. But this reasoning is flawed. Its conclusions are not a necessary outcome.

Churches have life cycles, just as economies have life cycles. Neighborhoods change. Unemployment and inflation move up and down. For this reason it is wise to approach congregational stewardship from a broader perspective.

A local church stands as the lighthouse in its community. The people who compose its membership reflect the reality of Christ throughout the week to their friends. While their gospel message will never change, the ministries they provide in a community may change as the community changes.

Generous stewardship is more about long-term viability than annual budgets. That is why churches are wise to develop a cradle-to-grave stewardship program. Children's participation should be warmly invited. Youth need to be givers, not just receivers. Younger adults need to make sure kingdom values are reflected in their financial priorities. And older adults should leave a legacy that will touch lives in future generations.

While each congregation will have a bottom-line budget number to support their anticipated ministries, many churches are discovering the

---

years of famine will follow them. . . . . And now let Pharaoh look for a discerning and wise man and put him in charge of the land of Egypt. Let Pharaoh appoint commissioners over the land to take a fifth of the harvest of Egypt during the seven years of abundance. They should collect all the food of these good years that are coming and store up the grain under the authority of Pharaoh, to be kept in the cities for food. This food should be held in reserve for the country, to be used during the seven years of famine that will come upon Egypt, so that the country may not be ruined by the famine" (Gen. 41:28–30, 33–36).

value of establishing foundations. These foundations are endowments, or future funds, to guarantee the underwriting of future ministry projects. I tell churches, "If ministry to your zip code is as important as you say it is, then you need enough money in reserve to run your ministry even in down economic conditions when portfolios shrink, inflation grows, or members lose employment." If we are to keep advancing the gospel of Christ, we must help people understand that generous stewardship is more about long-term viability than an annual budget.

Generous Stewardship Is More about Spending Money on Others than on Ourselves

When I say stewardship is more about spending money on others than ourselves, the issue is what percentage of our annual giving goes to programs inside the church versus programs outside the church. What percentage goes to evangelism and outreach, compared to edification and internal nurture? How many churches appear to outsiders as posh social clubs? How many highly paid church staffs are little more than institutional chaplains? How many elaborate church facilities house high-energy programs that do little more than keep our people out of the world?

By the very nature of things, Christian nurture is easier than Christian outreach. Evangelism is difficult because our culture is bent on pluralism and cool toward the church. Another thing is that Christians naturally prefer the fellowship of brothers and sisters in Christ to those outside the church who have little knowledge of and little interest in spiritual things. It is also true that Satan works very hard to make sure the infectious gospel is quarantined in isolation in our churches.

While Christian nurture is biblical—and therefore commendable— many churches have their Great Commission strategy backwards. We think if we just build up believers to some hypothetical spiritual level, they will reach out to others who do not know Christ. Unfortunately, however, the longer a Christian remains within the church, the fewer friends he or she has in the community. A better strategy is to nurture Christians through reaching the lost, versus trying to nurture Christians to reach the lost.

In heaven we will worship, learn, and live in community. The only thing we cannot do in heaven is bring lost people into the knowledge of Christ. Outreach must always be in the forefront of our Christian mission. As that is the case, so outreach must also be in the forefront of our budgets.

Following the example of Christ, we must fight these conditions. We must invest a growing portion (even a disproportion) of our investments in reaching those outside Christ, for generous stewardship is more about investing in others, than investing in ourselves.

Generous Stewardship Is More about Commitment than Capacity

We grow through sharing our abilities and resources with others. Generous investing, then, primarily is an issue of faithfulness, devotion, and dedication. Obviously, wealthy individuals are in a position to make large contributions. But their gifts are no more significant than the two small coins given by the poor widow reported in the gospel of Luke.[73]

Jesus taught that our values and money are woven together. We spend our money on the things that matter most to us. It should not surprise us, therefore, to find that congregations with healthy per capita giving are comprised of people deeply committed to the mission of the church. Their attitude is "Grace Church is *my* church," rather than "I

---

73   "As Jesus looked up, he saw the rich putting their gifts into the temple treasury. He also saw a poor widow put in two very small copper coins. 'Truly I tell you,' he said, 'this poor widow has put in more than all the others. All these people gave their gifts out of their wealth; but she out of her poverty put in all she had to live on'" (Luke 21:1–4).

attend Grace Church." Faithful members are more than attendees or observers—they are deeply vested owners, regardless of financial capacity.

Hoisting the Sails

Here are several specific ways to enhance stewardship awareness and practice in a congregation:

FINANCIAL STUDY IN HOME CELL GROUPS

Small groups can provide a warm learning environment for the study of a classic book like *Your Finances in Changing Times*,[74] or a video series such as *Financial Peace University*.[75] The typical advanced preparation, group discussion, and peer support of the cell format encourages a healthy accountability to practice the principles studied.

PREACHING SERIES ON *GROWING THROUGH GIVING*

Money is a huge and often unpleasant issue in most families. Avoiding this topic in preaching, however, is a big mistake, even when it is avoided so as not to offend people. People can discover freedom, release, and joy when they practice biblical principles of financial management. A positive message, avoiding an *ought* and *should* approach, is usually warmly accepted.

INVESTMENT SEMINARS

The Boomer age wave is now moving into retirement. Most of the seventy-six million Boomers already have a financial game plan underway, but many of them are unsure what their senior years' financial picture will actually look like. They have dumped money into 401Ks and IRAs, channeling most of it into the stock market. But as the retirement

---

74   Larry Burkett, *Your Finances in Changing Times* (Chicago: Moody Publishers, 1989).

75   https://www.daveramsey.com/fpu.

stage nears, they may prefer more diversified portfolios. Seminars led by credible Christian consultants with no vested interest can provide valuable information to our people. Similar seminars for middle-aged adults and even younger adults have also been well received.

STEWARDSHIP *FAITH STORIES*

Whether spoken from the pulpit, presented in a class, or shared in a small group, hearing real-life stories about people using their resources (including their time and finances) for kingdom purposes is highly motivational. Some individuals prefer their stories be passed on by someone else, to avoid any appearance of pride or to maintain their anonymity. Whatever the format, Christians need examples of ways to practice generous stewardship.

EMPLOYMENT COUNSELING

The capacity to give is directly related to one's job status. Vocational guidance and employment counseling can help our people better understand their marketable skills and assets and assist them in their job searches. A team of volunteers can head up this ministry, which is usually provided on a case-by-case, appointment basis.

DIRECT SOLICITATION OF MAJOR GIFTS

Professional development officers are soliciting funds from the people of your church on a regular basis. Yet for some reason, church leaders think it is unspiritual to request specific gifts from particular members. While caution is definitely in order here, and proper decorum is a must, occasions occur when inviting a targeted gift toward a ministry opportunity is most appropriate.

GIFTS OF STOCK

Some donors, but not very many, are aware of the tax implications of giving an appreciated stock to the church. Educating the congregation on the benefits to them and the Kingdom is important. If your church does not have an account with a broker, then set one up so that you are able to receive these types of gifts.

Special-Projects List

Younger givers are more responsive to target giving than storehouse tithing. ("Storehouse tithing" means congregants give one-tenth of their income directly to the church, and not to ministries or organizations outside the church, except for freewill offerings above the tithe.) While maintaining an emphasis on proportionate giving that supports the church's ministries, it is wise to also maintain a list of approved special projects that can be underwritten by those who have interest in them. Obviously, care must be exercised not to detract from a unified budget, but cautiously followed, this practice can draw gifts from newer donors, as well as highlight opportunities for extra gifts from those with extra capacity.

Ministry Highlights

As mentioned earlier, never take an offering without highlighting where that offering goes. It is not very motivating to be told your offering is being given to a budget, or it is supporting the church, or it is "meeting our needs." Rather, take every opportunity to relate how specific groups are being helped, built up, supported, or changed, through the congregation's generous giving. Briefly describe one particular ministry, and then always affirm your thankfulness for faithful giving to the church. After all, without faithful giving, no program and no vital ministry is possible.

Tax-Preparation Assistance and Financial Counseling

At tax time, many people are open to talking with a confidential advisor about their financial situation. Some who are living on the margin are open to counsel regarding budgetary changes, financial restructuring, or simply suggestions on where to channel their tax refund. A ministry team of accountants can help individuals practice better financial stewardship.

HOME-PURCHASE ADVISING

Establish a ministry team of non-realtors who can provide people with information on housing options in your community, including school systems and other local concerns. Individuals on the team can also offer objective feedback regarding "how much house" the inquirer may need or can afford. A committee such as this can certainly help young couples avoid the debt implications of overbuying.

CHAPTER 16

INVITING FACILITIES

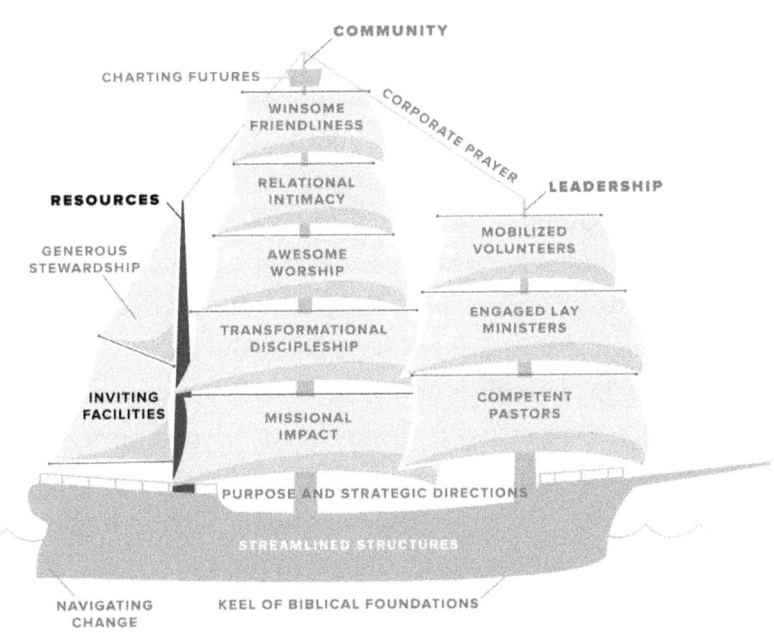

On the mast of resources is a second important sail called Inviting Facilities. A number of churches simply have too much facility, some because they built with too optimistic a view of their growth potential, and others because of steadily declining attendance. Some congregations rent the space where they gather because they do not want to be strapped with building debt. Many never plan to own property.

Dollars spent on buildings cannot be spent on staff and ministries. Therefore, maximizing space resources available to a congregation is critical.

Inviting Facilities Are More Multipurpose than Event-Specific

Two congregations presently renting space are nearing the time when they will acquire their own property. Rather than building an auditorium designed only for worship, both churches plan to construct a multipurpose facility. One pastor said their large group space would be called "the community center." They want a community center where neighborhood activities take first place and that will double as a worship center. To these pastors, this kind of facility makes more sense than constructing a typical worship facility. They never envision needing a single-use building.

Even for churches that have constructed large auditoriums, however, flexibility is still necessary and possible. Two well-known churches have similarly designed auditoriums, both pie-shaped, with each seating over 3,500 people. Both facilities have main-level seating, with approximately twenty concrete rows (with theater seats) ascending up around the perimeter. One church constructed their main level with a sloped floor and fixed seating. The other church chose a slightly higher platform, and a flat, level floor for the main part of the auditorium.

The first facility is used primarily for the church's weekend services and where they occasionally schedule performances by guest artists. The second church, with its flat floor and stacked-chair seating, is also used for weekend worship services, but in addition to that, it is available for many other functions—such as when Campus Crusade for Christ rents their space for marriage seminars. When community groups need workshop space, this church has the capacity to configure their space with tables and chairs.

The benefits of facilities offering flexible space is also observed by the way two other congregations built their educational space. One church built a two-story educational building with rectangular classrooms, all approximately 1,200 square feet. The second church erected a multistory, spacious educational facility, with no interior bearing walls. The rooms, like hotel ballrooms, can be expanded or reduced in size by the fifty-two-decibel portable walls that move on a track system. These examples show that the more adaptable our facilities are, the more likely they will be in use far into the future.

The question many pastors ask—"Do we have adequate facilities?"—can only be answered after church leaders determine what they want to accomplish. And a related issue is present in our current American environment: if in a postmodern world fewer people are coming to church campuses than to outside community events, having too much facility (once thought as an asset) may likely be a liability in the future.

Inviting Facilities Are More about Program Requirements than Ownership

This principle is similar to the principle considered above, yet it differs slightly. First Church has a classy room called "the Blue Room," approximately one thousand square feet in size, decorated and inhabited for years by the seniors' class. Over time, the class has dwindled down to a handful of people. Meanwhile, the church's youth program is growing, and could use a larger space. But because of a perceived "ownership," switching classrooms could not happen.

Another example is Christ Church, which has seen an influx of young families. On many weekends, they have as many as twenty-five four-year-olds, all jammed into a six-hundred-square-foot room. As their youth ministry is rather small, the obvious space solution is to give the group with the largest attendance the larger room. However, in many congregations (with stiff "rudders"), this suggestion would be met with resistance.

Understandably, most groups want their own place, and many even decorate and equip their space to their preferences. Nevertheless, stewardship of facilities requires a movement away from ownership, away from turf protection. Within reason, and where possible, effective churches flex with space according to current program needs

Inviting Facilities Are More about People-Care than Maximum Capacities

In our neighborhood, the local Target was leveled, and a new Target Superstore was constructed on the same property. Our local McDonald's (like thousands across the country) has undergone a face-lift. Perhaps most notably, the Minneapolis Metrodome was bulldozed so that the new Vikings' stadium could be built. These changes were made to attract people.

Churches also age over time and become less accommodating to cultural expectations. Who could blame a young couple who would rather place their preschooler in a fresh, attractive, age-appropriate facility, than in a drab room with what appears to be hand-me-down furnishings? When attendees pull into Church A, with potholes, grass growing up through cracks, and hard-to-discern parking stripes, what is their impression? When they pull into Church B, with a smooth seal coat, crisp parking stripes, and ample parking, will their impression be better? People-care, as it relates to facilities, means a church maintaining a clean, fresh appearance. Light bulbs are routinely replaced, carpets are regularly shampooed, and bathrooms are hygienically cleaned. Parking doesn't fall below a "1 space for every 2-2.5 people" ratio. Room space doesn't exceed the 80 percent capacity rule. Foyers are comfortable, with clear signage, and gracious hosts are available for assistance.

The main concern is not the highest number of people we can get onto our campus and into our programs. The real issue is how we can best attract people and care for them through the use of our facilities.

Hoisting the Sails

Multiple Services

Because of escalating construction costs, most churches will schedule additional services before building a larger auditorium. I have preached in churches that have up to six services per weekend. One West Coast congregation has eleven weekend options for church-goers to attend.

Video Venues

Jacob's Well offers five services to accommodate the two thousand-plus people drawn to their weekend services. Three services are in the main auditorium, and two services take place in their smaller chapel. Separate worship teams lead in the two venues. Since four of the services share two time slots, a live speaker is only present in the larger auditorium. Jacob's Well uses a video of the message, recorded earlier, for the two chapel services. A live band and less formal atmosphere make the chapel service appealing to many. In addition, the main speaker frequently drops into the chapel service to offer a greeting, make announcements, or offer the closing prayer.

Saturday Night Services

Some churches have tried a Saturday evening service, but then pulled the plug when it never gained traction with their people. But a growing number of congregations are experiencing good interest in this option, offering Saturday evening services, and even some Sunday night services, identical to the Sunday morning services.

Constance Church began a Saturday evening service, believing it would be a good venue for singles. To their surprise, many families with young children began to attend. They learned the families came because it was easier to get the children ready for church at 5:00 PM than it was to get them up early for the 9:00 AM service. Also, for many kids who play team sports, events in their community are usually scheduled on Sundays, making worship on Saturday a great family option.

Multisite

Many congregations have chosen not to relocate their growing church to a larger property. For one thing, the cost of simply replicating their present facilities on a larger property is wildly prohibitive, let alone the expense of adding additional buildings on the anticipated property. A growing number of churches have preferred following a new trend—getting bigger by remaining smaller. Eagle Brook Church, for example, offers a minimum of four services on each of their campuses. When they added their sixth campus (their goal is to have ten campuses), attendance topped twenty thousand at their twenty-six weekend services. Can you imagine the size of campus Eagle Brook would need to reach that many people on one property? (And think of the parking and egress issues that would have to be worked out for a campus of that size.) Eagle Brook is only one example of how a multisite approach to church growth can be highly successful. Scores of articles on multisite ministries are available on Leadership Network's Web site. The results of LeadNet's surveys of one thousand multisite congregations are also available online.[76]

Shared Space

Many churches have facility space, particularly classroom space, which remains empty during most of the week. Operators of private

---

76 www.leadnet.org.

schools, charter schools, Christian schools, and schools for mentally or physically challenged adults are very often looking to partner with a church or other organization that can help them keep expenses down.

Decentralized Ministry

Adult classrooms require between twelve and thirty square feet per pupil, depending on whether seating is in rows or around tables. To provide classrooms for three hundred adults in a discussion format would require nine thousand square feet, with up to ten classrooms. If you calculate the building cost for the classrooms, the cost to any church is significant. Instead, by using home groups for learning and community, expenses are almost nonexistent.

Removable Walls

I began this chapter by saying that maximizing space resources available to a congregation is critical. An example of maximizing space is Trinity Church, which years ago built a one-thousand-seat, semi-circular worship center, with non-bearing walls between the auditorium and its large foyer. The worship center was designed to expand to two thousand seats by simply removing the drywall rear walls.

Church Mergers

Over the past decade I have seen a growing number of churches merge with other congregations. Frequently, one church has a stronger ministry in one or more areas, and the congregation willing to join with this stronger church has its challenges. Churches desire merger with another congregation for many different reasons. Some have lost critical membership. Because of debt level, some churches anticipate losing their property to a bank. Sometimes healthy churches that have not experienced a loss of membership or a challenging debt level still choose to join their efforts with others to become, in the words of Tomberlin and Bird, "Better Together."[77]

---

[77] Jim Tomberlin and Warren Bird, *Better Together: Making Church Mergers Work* (San Francisco: Jossey-Bass Books, 2012).

CHAPTER 17

NEXT STEPS

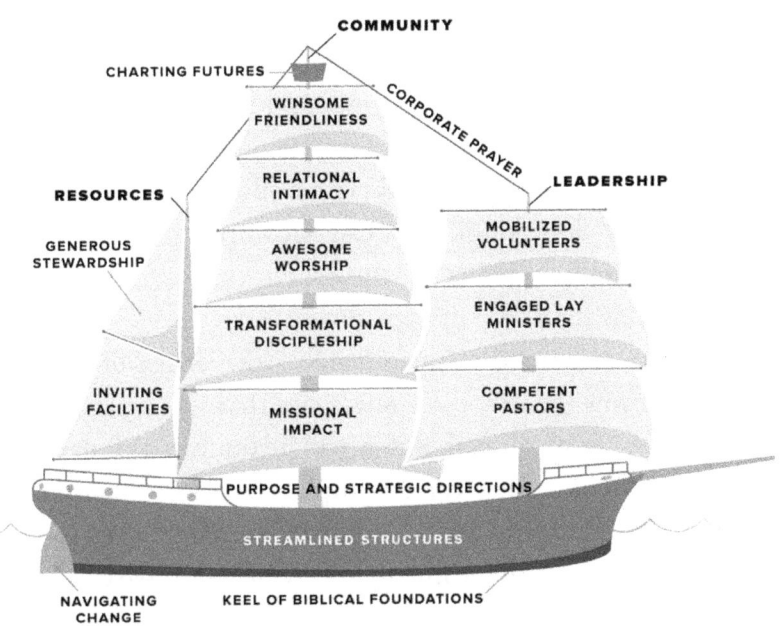

When I help churches determine their "next steps," I use a "Church Health Assessment" tool developed by Ministry Transitions, Inc., to delineate sixteen church health factors (see Appendix C). Next to each factor is a place for the workshop participants to rank from 1 to 10 how well their church is doing. Then I collect all data sheets, add factor totals, divide them by the number of participants, and arrive at a mean score (average) generated for each dimension of church health.

In other words, if "mobilized volunteers" receives an average of 5, then that sail is half way up. Maybe a church comes out with a 7.5 in the area of worship. Then that sail is 75 percent full.

After mean scores are calculated, I advise churches to identify three or four of the sixteen ministry factors, and brainstorm ways to hoist the sails—in other words, to strengthen that area of ministry. For example, I encourage them to think of ways they could do a better job of enfolding people into the church (relational intimacy), or doing a better job of strengthening the church's outreach (missional impact).

A team of people with expertise in a selected area discusses problems and identifies solutions to improve that dimension of ministry. When I ask the teams to come up with forty or fifty ways to strengthen their area of ministry, they often look at me like a deer in the headlights. Typically, they don't think they can accomplish this goal, but teams working diligently together for the benefit of the church can generate more solutions than they first imagined.

With the list of ways to strengthen a particular area of ministry before them, the teams identify three outcomes that will be accomplished in 90 days, three more outcomes that will be done in 180 days, and three additional outcomes they can accomplish by the end of 360 days.

With 90, 180, and 360-day outcomes selected, implementation teams can then work on the initiative for which they have been recruited. One team, for example, might want to strengthen relational intimacy. With their list of projects (outcomes), they can brainstorm who could be on the sub-teams to take responsibility for completing the project by its deadline. Another team can assemble a group of six people to pull off four quarterly dinners. Another team could accept responsibility for starting two new Bible studies, one beginning in three months and one starting in nine months.

A delicate balance is needed when building the ministry (implementation) teams. If a congregation wants to hoist the worship sail, why not simply assign it to the people presently responsible for worship? On the face of it, that might sound reasonable. But if some people have already been in charge of the worship area and it needs improvement, perhaps additional, knowledgeable, outside members should compose that project team in order to bring a fresh perspective.

Church health is not about a ten-year plan; it is about clarifying the direction a church wants to go and then trimming the sails on an ongoing basis. This year a congregation addresses these initiatives; next year they have another opportunity to tweak other sails.

When this process is operational, people feel empowered. They realize they are not victims, nor is the health of the church only the pastor's concern. The model shows them that competent pastoring is but one of the factors. They realize they can set up a team to assess how their community is changing, and they can become change agents in strengthening areas of ministry to meet community needs. They have a say in their church's future.

WHERE DO WE GO FROM HERE?

So where do we go from here? I suggest pastors guide key church leaders through a discussion of this book. These would be the movers and shakers, whether presently on a church board or not. After understanding the sixteen factors, lead them through the assessment exercise. Next, select the ministry areas (church health factors) that need strengthening. Then assemble the right people to select initiatives. Finally, assign specific responsibilities to those best equipped for successful completion of the initiatives.

After a study of the sixteen health factors, leaders begin understanding that church health is not a mystery. There are reasons some churches are growing, just as there are reasons some are not. Some variables are out of our control, such as the growth rate or decline rate of our neighborhood. But much is, in fact, in our control!

Our church's future will be determined by how well we attend to people outside the faith community, how well we can draw them into our discipleship community, and how well we can help them mature to become part of a ministry team that serves others. When we do this, we will experience our church at its best!

APPENDIX A

SHIP MODEL FOR CHURCH HEALTH

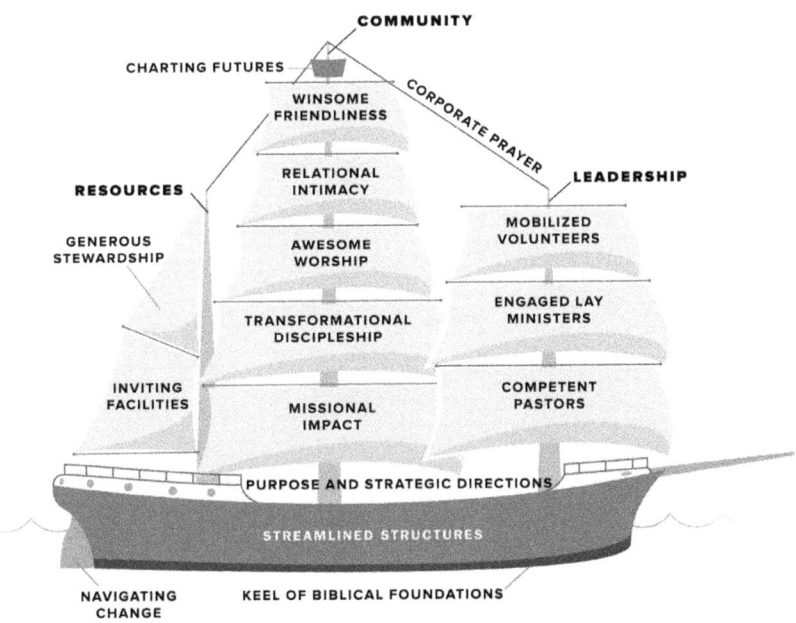

© Ministry Transitions, Inc., 1996.

APPENDIX B

Ways to Support and Recognize Volunteers

Take volunteers out for coffee to thank them for a particular job.

Pay for volunteers to attend a training conference.

Give them a weekly call to ask how they are doing.

Put on a surprise "thank you" party.

Work a volunteer's story into sermon illustrations.

Provide substitutes for all leaders and teachers.

Invite each volunteer out to lunch at least once a year.

Organize class members in buying a surprise gift.

Write brief sketches about volunteers for the newsletter.

Use a team approach in ministry.

Schedule fellowship times outside of actual service time.

Know and address all volunteers by first name.

Pay an informal social call to volunteers and their families.

Ask outgoing volunteers to consult from time to time.

Give a genuine touch of care—a pat on the back.

Have students write notes of thanks to their leaders.

Never eschew positive communication from the pulpit.

Allow ownership for the program in which they are involved.

Keep abreast of each volunteer's personal life.

Make flexible schedules.

Allow a period of orientation and training.

Write a song or a poem expressing appreciation.

Make sure they are not overworked.

Have prayer partners.

Present flowers to volunteers on "Shared-Ministry Sunday."

Provide special mementos or recognition.

Ask their needs.

Make a small budget available.

Do an entire newsletter yearly on just volunteers.

Arrange a volunteer "night out" with free child care, tickets, or gift cards.

Provide choice parking places.

Give gift certificates from restaurants.

Use carnations to identify staff on "Volunteer Sunday."

Pray for volunteers during the worship service.

Encourage the congregation to express its gratitude to volunteers.

Treat them as experts on their class.

Allow a testimony time on how the volunteer has ministered to others.

Find a boat they can borrow to go water skiing.

Provide a cabin where they can get away.

Provide Web links to information helpful to a volunteer's task.

Quickly respond to their requests and concerns.

Compliment them to other church members.

Provide a pictorial history of the volunteer in action.

Provide an annual recognition luncheon or banquet.

Offer an affirmative touch.

Respond to their concerns.

Send fruit baskets at Christmas, a turkey at Thanksgiving, and so on.

Give a gift to their children.
Have them into your home for a meal.

APPENDIX C

CHURCH HEALTH ASSESSMENT

© 1996 Ministry Transitions, Inc

Assign a score to each church health factor based on the descriptions and explanation presented in *Your Church at Its Best*. Use a 10-point scale, with one (1) being extremely poor and ten (10) being outstanding.

Part 1: STRUCTURAL INTEGRITY

Biblical Foundations _____

Vision and Strategic Directions _____

Streamlined Structures _____

Charting Futures _____

Navigating Change _____

Corporate Prayer _____

Part 2: LEADERSHIP

Mobilized Volunteers _____

Engaged Lay Leaders _____

Effective Pastors _____

Part 3: COMMUNITY

Winsome Friendliness _____

Relational Intimacy _____

Awesome Worship _____

Transformational Discipleship _____

Missional Impact _____

Part 4: RESOURCES

Generous Stewardship _____

Inviting Facilities _____

About the Authors

JOHN R. CIONCA, Ph.D., is executive director of Ministry Transitions, Inc., a Christian ministry dedicated to helping church leaders and churches plan their future, and emeritus professor of ministry leadership at Bethel Seminary in St. Paul, Minnesota. He graduated from Elmhurst College (B.A.) and Denver Seminary (M.R.E.). He then earned the M.A. and Ph.D. degrees from Arizona State University. Dr. Cionca has served as a lead pastor, interim pastor, youth pastor, minister of education, seminar leader, and transitions coach. He has advised over five hundred pastors and ministry leaders and has consulted with nearly three hundred congregations. John is the author or editor of ten books, including *Before You Move: A Guide to Making Transitions in Ministry*, *Dear Pastor: Ministry Advice from Seasoned Pastors*, *Search Counsel: A Devotional Coaching Guide for Call Committees*, *Solving Church Education's Ten Toughest Problems*, and *Teamship: 52 Inspirational Readings for Leaders*. John and his wife, Barbara, live in Arden Hills, Minnesota, and Mesa, Arizona. They enjoy golf, hiking, reading, and especially hanging with their Grand Kiddos.

If you have questions on this book, or if you would like to talk with Dr. Cionca about the factors contributing to congregational health, you may contact him at 651.335.5836 or jrcionca@gmail.com.

Leonard G. Goss led editorial efforts at B&H Publishing Group, Crossway Books, Zondervan Publishing House/HarperCollins Publishers, Mott Publishers, and the Evangelical Book Club. He began his publishing career with John Wiley & Sons, and now with his wife operates GoodEditors.com, a boutique editorial services firm (www.goodeditors.com). Len is the author of *A Brief Style Guide to Good Writing for Authors and Editors* and *A Guide for Authors, Editors, and Proofreaders in the Preparation of Manuscripts*. With his wife, Carolyn, he has authored *The Little Style Guide to Great Christian Writing and Publishing,* and with Don M. Aycock he has authored *The Little Handbook to Perfecting the Art of Christian Writing, Writing Religiously, The Christian Writer's Book,* and *Inside Religious Publishing*. His own faith story is included in the books *Mere Christians* and *In Their Own Words*. He is recognized with biographical reference listings in many volumes, including *Who's Who in the Media and Communications, Who's Who in Religion,* and *Notable American Men*. Born in San Diego, California, he and Carolyn now live in the Valley of the Sun. He earned the B.A. degree from Arizona State University, the M.A. degree from the University of Windsor, and the M.Div. degree from Trinity Evangelical Divinity School of Trinity International University. The thing he enjoys most is spending time with his four beautiful granddaughters—Lia, Maddie, Sylvie, and Shelby. His dog, Tim, is better than other dogs.

ORDER INFORMATION

To order additional copies of this book, please visit
www.redemption-press.com.
Also available on Amazon.com and BarnesandNoble.com
Or by calling toll free 1-844-2REDEEM.

CPSIA information can be obtained
at www.ICGtesting.com
Printed in the USA
FFHW021354050119
50063985-54884FF